PRIVATE EQUITY MASTERY

Praise for *Private Equity Mastery*

"A must-read! *Private Equity Mastery* opens the private equity black box. It makes complex ideas about private equity transparent and easily understandable. Foye has literally created a how-to guide on all dimensions of the PE universe. Ignore at your own risk."

—JOSEPH V. TRIPODI, former Chief Marketing Officer of The Coca-Cola Company, MasterCard, Subway, Allstate, and Seagram's

"Groundbreaking! *Private Equity Mastery* is for the rest of us (who don't work at a private equity firm). It does a masterful job of explaining the inner workings, nuances, and watchouts of private equity for the investor, executive, or entrepreneur."

—DON KNAUSS, Chairman, McKesson Corporation; former Chairman and CEO, The Clorox Company

"A masterstroke! Finally, a book that demystifies private equity in an easy-to-understand way. I wish I had this book before I started my journey as a board member for public and PE-backed companies. *Private Equity Mastery* explains how private equity works, what drives its outcomes, and how to plan and execute effectively to maximize opportunities when engaging with PE firms."

—DR. AJAI PURI, Non-Executive Director at Fresh Del Monte Produce, Inc., IMI PLC, Olam Group Limited, and Califia Farms LP

"Don't let this book pass you by. Anyone who invests or is interested in investing should read this book. Private equity investing has its own unique profile, challenges, and nuances as an asset class, which are rarely understood by the average investor. *Private Equity Mastery* will prepare you for the opportunity and improve your chances of success."

—KEVIN ROBERTS, Investment Advisor

Private Equity Mastery

The Ultimate Playbook for Investors, Executives, and Entrepreneurs

ROBERT FOYE

AUTHOR.INC

A\
AUTHOR.INC

Private Equity Mastery

Edited by David Caissie

Cover design by Pete Garceau

Interior design by Zoe Norvell

ISBN: Hardcover: 978-1-966372-07-3

Paperback: 978-1-966372-06-6

Published by Author.Inc

Printed in the United States of America

First Edition: December 2025

For more information, visit: RobertFoye.com

To Kristi, Robert, William,
Meredith, and Annabel—

who make everything I do possible,
even if they don't always know it.

TABLE OF CONTENTS

PART II
Survive and Thrive in a PE Portfolio Company
87

PART III
Win in PE as an Investor or Seller
185

"The test of a first-rate intelligence is the ability to hold two opposed ideas in the mind at the same time and still retain the ability to function."

— F. SCOTT FITZGERALD

Why I Wrote This Book

My name is Robert Foye. I didn't start in private equity. I earned my stripes the hard way. After a thirty-year career across multiple industries, I pivoted into PE, bringing decades of hard-won experience as both an operator and investor. I've spent over three decades investing across stocks, bonds, real estate, and now private equity. What I share in this book isn't theory: it's what I've lived. I'm also teaching this material to the next generation of investors as an adjunct professor for MBA students at the University of Houston, with plans to expand to other universities in the US, UK, and Hong Kong.

When I was in my late thirties, I worked as a mid-level manager at the Coca-Cola Company in Europe. I had many conversations with my colleagues about private equity. The gist of our musings was how we would like to finish our corporate careers in our forties and then work for a PE company running one of their consumer products portfolio companies. The plan was to ditch the corporate hamster wheel, storm into PE, and self-actualize in the immense value we could create. Of course, we only had a vague concept of what PE actually was. To us, it was "capitalism on steroids" where sharp, seasoned executives like us (somewhat exaggerated) could run companies freely and make changes quickly. We would be undeterred and unfettered by the usual checks and balances of corporate bureaucracy.

After all, we knew how to build businesses—gain customers, drive innovation, grow market share, lead teams, and manage people. Under PE ownership, we would be free to hire and fire at will and implement what really matters to consumers and customers at a much faster pace. And of course, we would build significant wealth along the way.

But we had no real understanding of how private equity firms actually work—what drives them and how they define success. We had no experience or knowledge base to rely on, and how could we? We were like teenagers reading Victorian novels about love, dreaming of mastery in a world we had no experience in. It was all concept and theory with no grounding in reality.

Fast-forward a few years later in my forties, my Morgan Stanley investment advisor, eyeing my portfolio, suggested I invest a significant amount into private equity for "enhanced returns and diversification." (I'm a big believer in low-cost passive index funds, but yes I still have an investment advisor—that's a story for another book.)

What could possibly go wrong? I had multi-decades of experience investing in stocks, bonds, and real estate. Wasn't private equity just another asset class? I made the investment, once again with only a surface-level understanding of what private equity actually entailed. If only I had this book back then, I would have been a better investor.

Private equity has a completely different risk, return, and liquidity profile compared to stocks and bonds. Fully understanding it can significantly enhance your portfolio and investment decisions.

Fast-forward again to my mid-fifties. I was offered the role of CEO of a one-billion-dollar PE-portfolio company owned by Carlyle. I accepted the challenge and ran the company for five years. Had I possessed a clearer, more detailed understanding of how private equity operates, I would have been a far more effective executive.

Managing a private equity portfolio company involves different objectives, priorities, and pace than leading a public company. Understanding these nuances can lead to significantly higher overall success rates.

Meanwhile, the PE fund I had invested in a decade ago still hadn't wound down. I'm left with murky updates and no clear line of sight on my investment returns. In the investment world, they call this low liquidity and limited transparency.

And along the way with my investment and management time, I noticed another very important trend—private equity has steadily captured a larger share of the overall company universe. It has now become a juggernaut. Today, there are more than five times as many PE-owned companies as there were twenty-five years ago. At the same time, PE has begun the process of making aggressive inroads into everyday individual retirement accounts like 401(k)s and IRAs. Soon, even small retail investors will be able to include private equity funds in their portfolios.

Once focused mainly on large-cap companies, private equity now buys, builds, and exits investments across the spectrum, from mom-and-pop rollups to mid-cap firms and industry giants. What was once the exclusive domain of elite, sophisticated institutional investors like endowments and pension funds is quickly becoming accessible to everyday investors.

Private equity is having its mainstream moment.

I know there are many people like me (PE investors, executives stepping into portfolio companies, or business owners considering a sale) who have only a vague understanding of how PE really works. As I often say, private equity is a black box: we can watch it from the outside, but we rarely see inside or fully understand the consequences of how it's operating.

That's why I wrote this book.

This book isn't for private equity insiders (although those considering a career in PE may still find it helpful). Insiders receive specific, detailed training and experience in fundraising, portfolio management, deal execution, and driving operational performance. This book is for everyone else:

- Retail investors ready to diversify their portfolios beyond stocks and bonds for higher returns and more diversification.
- Industry executives and C-suite leaders itching to make a move to a PE-backed role to show their true mettle.
- Small to midsize business owners who might one day be approached by a PE firm to sell their business for a big paycheck (and likely stay on for a time post-sale).
- Curious business minds, students, and professionals who want to crack the code on how private equity actually works.

I have scoured countless books and articles on PE, but none cut through the noise to deliver a clear end-to-end breakdown of the model—what drives PE firms, what good looks like, and what pitfalls to avoid. This book aims to do just that.

I have tried to combine the most relevant academic research with my own leadership and investment experience to offer a comprehensive, easy-to-read guide into the world of private equity. If

I've done my job right, this book rips open and reveals the black box that is private equity.

The stakes have never been higher—and the opportunities never greater. Time to step up and master the game.

—ROBERT FOYE
Houston, Texas. November 2025.

INTRODUCTION

I once overheard a deal unravel in real time.

The founder thought he was selling for freedom, but six months later, he was sidelined. His team was scattered, and the acquirer gutted the company he built.

The absolute worst situation you can find yourself in is making a major decision about your business or your money without the knowledge and experience to evaluate what you're doing.

Ignorance destroys outcomes, whether it's about the time you spend working in a company or the money you invest.

I've seen business owners sell to private equity, only to be ousted six months later. They lose equity, lose earned income, and sit there scratching their heads: "What just happened? Everything I know about doing business has been turned upside down."

It's because they didn't understand the private equity process, who they were dealing with, and what they should have looked out for from the beginning.

Private equity feels like a black box. To most founders, you fear losing control. As an executive, you scramble to meet new expectations you never saw coming. As an investor, you jump in late, confused by jargon and structure that no one explains.

You sense the power of private equity everywhere. It's in headlines about layoffs, in stories of transformed companies, in whispers about astronomical returns and executive payouts. But you don't understand the rules. You watch from the outside while private equity firms control all the information. They understand how the process works. They drive everything on their terms.

Meanwhile, you're left in the dark. Whether you're a business owner considering a sale, an investor seeking returns, or an operator trying to lead a portfolio company, you don't have the same access to information as the PE companies about how private equity actually works. You don't know what drives these firms. You don't understand how to succeed in their environment.

The world is shifting beneath your feet. Private equity is growing in influence, becoming a major part of the total business and investment landscape. It's creeping into retirement plans, into public markets, into every corner of the economy. That influence will only increase.

If you ignore private equity, you're ignoring a vast opportunity set: for selling your business, for greater investment returns and diversification, and for professional growth in managing and scaling companies. Without understanding how it works, you're paralyzed. Stuck between fear and opportunity. Between the caricatures and the reality.

You need clarity. You need real understanding of how private equity works, why it matters, and how to engage with it effectively, not propaganda defending or condemning it.

You need to push for better outcomes instead of being pushed around by forces you don't comprehend.

The Power To Play On Your Terms

This book shows how to engage with private equity on your terms. Whether you're building, selling, joining, or investing, you'll gain the fluency to protect what matters and the tools to turn pressure into leverage. No longer will you sit at the end of the table on the other side of private equity operators and not understand what's going on in the private equity game. Now you will be as educated as they are and you will understand the rules, the pressure points, what works, what doesn't, and what you need to do to succeed.

What You'll Learn

- Why private equity is no longer a niche. It's the dominant force shaping modern business.
- What PE really is and how it operates across a full investment cycle.
- What PE firms really want and what they don't care about.
- How deals are structured, negotiated, and sometimes unraveled.
- How to position you and your team before PE does it for you.
- How to negotiate better compensation terms and improved management equity plans (MEPs) if you join a PE-owned firm.
- What drives PE firm behavior post-close and how to adapt fast.
- How to spot and avoid the traps hidden in valuation, due diligence, and term sheets.

- What private equity means for investors at every level, from institutions to individuals.
- How to invest in private equity sensibly.
- How to increase your chances of success when selling your business to private equity, in terms of the valuation and your future role, equity, and earnout.
- Why private credit is becoming the new PE and why it matters so much when dealing with PE.

Private equity isn't evil, elusive, or elite. It's structured power with unstoppable upward momentum. When you understand how it moves, you can move with it or even ahead of it.

The numbers tell a story most people miss. More than 85% of companies in the US with revenue over $100 million are privately owned. Within that, there are now over 11,000 US companies owned by private equity, up from just 2,000 in the late 1990s. Meanwhile, the US public market has shrunk 40% over the same period, from 7,300 to about 4,300 companies.[1] If you're not fluent in PE, you're blind to where capital, talent, and power are flowing, and you risk being left behind.

This isn't some niche corner of finance anymore. Private equity is entering your 401(k)s, IRAs, and retail retirement platforms. Blackstone and others are partnering with Fidelity to integrate PE into everyday investor portfolios. The SEC is already examining this shift, and within six months, these investments will likely start appearing in retirement accounts everywhere. If you

---

1   Torsten Sløk, "Many More Private Firms in the US," Apollo Academy, April 20, 2024, https://www.apolloacademy.com/many-more-private-firms-in-the-us.

don't understand how PE works, you could be exposed to high-fee, low-transparency products without knowing it.

I've seen this transformation firsthand. Private equity gets terrible press: job losses, bankruptcies, and asset stripping. Yes, those happen. But PE also executes vital functions that keep capitalism healthy: restructuring companies during critical cycles, reallocating labor and capital to more productive uses, and generating financial returns that fuel new innovation. The real tragedy is when people write off the entire industry without understanding it.

When you truly grasp private equity, you operate with insider information and conviction. You make better investment decisions. You know which PE firms and opportunities to pursue and work with. You exit at higher valuations. This knowledge translates directly to results: 30%–100% higher annual earnings potential, better portfolio returns with less risk, and 20%–40% more when selling your business.

Fear moves to action when you open the black box. Your opportunity set expands dramatically. Private equity is here to stay and is having its breakthrough moment, not just in the shift from public to private companies, but in its move into mainstream investing. You can influence it, innovate within it, and maybe even make it better. But first, you need to understand it.

Ignore PE at your peril. The stakes have never been higher and the opportunity never greater. It's time to level up and play to win.

How Private Equity Evolved (1960s–Today)

Private equity may feel like a modern invention, but its roots stretch back decades. The earliest leveraged buyouts in the US appeared in the 1960s and 1970s, but the industry didn't truly take off until the 1980s. Deals like KKR's takeover of RJR Nabisco, immortalized in *Barbarians at the Gate*, defined the era. These early LBOs were fueled by junk bonds, aggressive leverage, and a "slash-and-burn" reputation. Many of those deals ended badly, but they cemented PE's identity as a powerful force in corporate restructuring.

By the 1990s and early 2000s, the industry had matured. Funds became institutionalized, pension and endowment money poured in, and firms began hiring operators and consultants to professionalize portfolio management. Private equity evolved into a model that combined leverage with operational improvement, no longer just about financial engineering.

The 2008 financial crisis tested the industry. Some firms collapsed under debt, but the survivors emerged stronger, armed with larger funds and more diversified strategies. Since then, PE has become mainstream, with trillions under management and a growing share of corporate ownership.

Globally, private equity has followed different paths. In Europe, PE often faced more regulatory scrutiny and cultural resistance, especially around labor laws and corporate governance. Still, it has grown into a major force in the UK, Germany, and the Nordics. In Asia, PE initially focused on growth capital rather than leveraged buyouts, especially in China and India where debt markets were less developed. Today, Asia is one of the fastest-growing PE regions, though it remains more fragmented and politically sensitive. Emerging markets in Africa and Latin America have seen slower adoption, with deals concentrated in consumer goods, infrastructure, and financial services.

This global spread matters because PE is not practiced the same way everywhere. A US buyout firm may rely heavily on leverage and multiple expansion, while an Asian growth fund might focus on minority stakes and expansion capital. European firms may put more emphasis on ESG (environmental, social, governance) to satisfy regulators and investors, while Latin American firms wrestle with political instability and currency risk. For investors, sellers, and managers, understanding these differences is critical. A one-size-fits-all view of private equity misses the nuances.

The bottom line is that private equity is no longer a US-centric phenomenon or a niche asset class. It is now a global model of ownership that influences industries, communities, and economies worldwide. While the tools may be similar—capital, leverage, and operational change—the way PE plays out depends heavily on local markets, regulations, and investor expectations. That history helps explain why today's PE firms look more sophisticated than the "barbarians" of the 1980s, but the incentives underneath haven't changed.

We have started where most people first feel the shift—the surge in PE. We've explained why private equity isn't going anywhere and why knowing its rise gives you the edge to act before others even see the wave. In the first chapter, we will see what matters most to PE firms, what really drives them, and how they operate across a full investment cycle. This brings us back to what PE firms really want: EBITDA and cash flow.

Our story begins there.

PART I

INSIDE THE BLACK BOX— UNDERSTAND HOW PE REALLY WORKS

"When you understand something, you don't fear it as much."

—MARIE CURIE

(PARAPHRASED)

CHAPTER 1

What PE Firms Are and What They Want

I thought a great brand or inspiring culture would win them over, only to watch their eyes light up at EBITDA and cash flow.

As a seasoned executive, I thought it was simple to build businesses—create a culture where people drive performance, focus everyone externally on the customer and the consumer, and innovate like crazy. If you do that, you win in business and you win in private equity. What I didn't fully grasp were the core metrics that truly drive PE firms.

In this chapter, I'll pull back the curtain on how PE firms actually work and what they truly care about. Fundraising (obtaining new investment funds from investors) provides the blood in the veins of private equity. Once the funds are in hand, then two simple metrics drive ruthless, high-stakes decisions across billion-dollar deals and investment funds. Great executives know that incentives shape behavior and ultimately drive business decisions. When you understand the incentives behind private equity, you see why they act the way they do—and why their approach to business differs so sharply from that of most executives.

A Short Primer On Private Equity

Private equity involves taking ownership stakes in private companies or taking public companies private, with the goal of improving performance and eventually realizing a return through an exit (selling the ownership to someone else). Unlike public-market investors, PE firms take an active role in management and strategic decisions. And they are on a much shorter value creation timeframe (more on that later).

In traditional retail investing, individuals or entities buy shares of publicly traded companies, giving them a small ownership stake. Beyond limited voting rights, they have no influence over key aspects like capital structure, management decisions, value-creation strategies, or exit timing. In contrast, private equity involves intense active ownership. The PE firm typically takes control of the portfolio company's strategic and financial direction: how it's financed, managed, and when it's ultimately sold.

At its core, PE is about value creation—acquiring companies with potential, improving them operationally or strategically, increasing returns through financial leverage, and exiting at a higher valuation.

Private equity frequently is given a bad rap due to its cost-cutting and use of leverage (which can lead to more frequent bankruptcies and financial restructurings). But it also serves a core function in capitalism—reallocating capital and labor, and driving companies through needed efficiency cycles. PE isn't inherently bad; it's a system that plays an important role, and like any system, it can be improved.

The Fundraising-Returns Feedback Loop

PE begins with and cares deeply about fundraising—not so much as a metric, but as the ultimate measure of their success. That's where the money comes to make the whole machine work.

Two things are intricately related and drive everything: fundraising and returns on investments. First PE raises the money to invest. Then if they can report good returns, fundraising becomes much easier, and the amounts raised become much larger. If returns are poor, fundraising dries up and it's more difficult to keep the machine rolling. Once you grasp the fundraising process, the mechanics of returns, and the importance of timing—especially the need for quick exits to make those returns work—the rest falls into place. It shapes everything from the company's culture to the pace of value creation and the urgency of execution.

Think about the cycle in simple terms: Once a PE firm raises money for a fund, they get paid; once they deliver high returns, they get paid a lot more, and they get significantly more money for the next cycle.

The Machine Behind The Money

You need to understand the machine behind the money for PE firms. They don't just buy companies. They start by raising hundreds of millions or billions of dollars from investors, and the clock is already ticking even as they take in money. A general partner (GP–the PE firm(s) and their employees) raises capital from investors, which are known as limited partners (LPs). These investors include pension funds, endowments, and high-net-worth family offices (soon to also include retail investors) into a ten-year fund.

The PE firm's survival depends on getting two things right: raising the next fund and delivering strong reported net returns after fees. They earn 2% annually on committed capital and 20% on profits, called carry interest (or just carry), above an 8% hurdle rate (minimum return for the carry to kick in). Capital isn't handed over all at once. Limited partners commit and the general partners call it (use the capital) as the deals arise. Every decision traces back to those two absolutes. If fundraising falters or reported returns lag, the firm's reputation erodes, capital dries up, and the machine grinds to a halt. That's why speed, leverage, and disciplined returns aren't just strategy, they're survival.

The Aggressive Hunt: From Capital To Exit

Once the capital is raised through fundraising, the machine shifts into an aggressive hunt: find, buy, improve, and sell fast. The timing and the clock are always ever-present and ever-important. Deal sourcing for new deals comes from auctions, relationships, or niche specializations developed by the firm. After screening, they launch deep due diligence in financial, legal, and operational areas, and they structure the deal with a mix of equity and debt. This is a leveraged buyout (LBO).

Once acquired, the PE firm manages every aspect of the company. They professionalize leadership, install KPIs (key performance indicators, or metrics), squeeze costs, expand revenues, and push operational upgrades. Every decision in a company buyout is measured against the exit. The average holding period is three to seven years but can extend to ten years plus. If results aren't showing by year two or three, pressure greatly intensifies. Once the clock starts ticking and a deal is made, it's imperative that the PE firm sees results in EBITDA (earnings before interest, taxes, depreciation, and amortization—to be explained in detail later) and cash flow, even in as little as six months or a year. If those measures aren't going in the right direction, pressure increases accordingly.

The Metrics That Really Matter

The metrics that matter to a PE firm related to running a portfolio company is EBITDA and cash flow. The reason is simple: there's a specific timeline that a PE firm has in mind when they buy and later sell (exit) a company. That timeline determines their internal rate of return (return on investment). To make the model work, firms that buy companies at a stated EBITDA multiple also need to sell them at a forecasted, target EBITDA multiple on exit. Whether that multiple holds depends largely on how much cash the business generates while it's being run. That cash isn't just reinvested—it also funds fees, dividends, and other obligations. So EBITDA and cash flow together are the metrics that PE firms care most about in order to report good, solid returns on their investments in portfolio companies.

When Great Performance Doesn't Matter

Culture, innovation, and brand often mean little to PE firms if they don't directly move EBITDA and cash flow. You can grow market share, win on the shelf, and succeed with customers and consumers—but if EBITDA and cash flow aren't rising, you will still face intense pressure under the private equity model. The PE firm's two real priorities are raising money and delivering portfolio returns, not perception or prestige.

The importance of raising money keeps the machine going over time. Delivering portfolio returns quickly, driven by increases in EBITDA and cash flow, becomes ever more important in a circular loop that comes back and helps with more fundraising. If you pitch vision before numbers—talking strategy without showing results—you fall off the radar of private equity firms. They lead with EBITDA and cash flow, and so must you. The strategy only matters when it's framed in measurable value: how EBITDA and cash flow can grow, quarter after quarter, year after year. Start with the numbers, then wrap your strategy around them—not the other way around.

I once worked with a Chief Financial Officer (CFO) who believed every metric mattered and spent enormous energy tracking them all. After a few years, he realized that in every meeting only two numbers truly dominated the conversation: EBITDA and cash flow. If those weren't moving in the right direction, nothing else really mattered.

This isn't just a preference for PE; it's their filter. The PE model has a ruthless simplicity to it. What looks like strategic oversight and business building is often just financial gravity. The formula is fairly straightforward: buy low, grow or cut, and exit high. Everything else is noise. If you misread this lens, you risk misaligned pitches, failed partnerships, or missed opportunities. You have to shape your narrative to match their key decision-making framework, or you'll be cut before the due diligence begins.

The Timing Trap: When Vision Meets Reality

Once you grasp the importance of EBITDA, cash-flow growth, the exit, and the ticking clock, you understand how private equity works. Everything flows from there—strong returns delivered quickly, which in turn drive successful fundraising.

I once joined a PE pitch that centered on a bold reinvention—global brand expansion, a rebuilt organization, and a long-term strategy to win with customers and consumers. But the PE team skipped past it and zeroed in on one thing: cash flow. "How do we increase it now? We don't have time for multi-year bets that may or may not pay off." I later saw the same dynamic play out inside a portfolio company. Management proposed heavy investments over two to three years, with returns expected in years four through six. But from the PE firm's perspective, they were already in year four of the deal, while the new CEO was only in year one. The investments—marketing, brand rebuilding, global expansion—were front-loaded and risky, with payback stretching into years seven, eight, and nine. That was simply too far beyond the firm's timeframe.

The investments were scaled back. Instead of a bold brand reinvention, the approach became incremental—smaller changes, less innovation—but aligned with the firm's timeline and its focus on EBITDA and cash flow.

Running A Marathon At A Sprint's Pace

I've talked to many CEOs of PE-portfolio companies, and they describe working with private equity owners as running a marathon at a sprint's pace.

Every quarter is a test—a chance to prove progress toward the finish line. You must show steady gains in EBITDA and cash flow. Even with a strong narrative and solid operating metrics, without those two numbers, nothing else matters.

Take the example of the CEO who became a portfolio company's second leader in just two years, after the first hire post-acquisition failed. By then, the investment was already in year three. For the new CEO, it was a fresh start; for the PE firm, the clock was ticking on what was meant to be a three-to-five-year flip, now stretched to five to seven. That raised the stakes: they expected proof of EBITDA and cash-flow growth every quarter. Any slip—one or two quarters off track—meant the pressure intensified, with heavier reporting, more scrutiny, and constant demands for alternative paths to boost results.

What seems like a ninety-day or one-hundred-eighty-day sprint is repeated over and over and is actually a three- or four-year marathon. The exit timeline brings timing pressure to everything you do; it makes that marathon look like a bunch of ninety-day sprints, and it becomes critical to stay on top and keep showing evidence of success toward the exit.

Mastering Both Sides Of The Equation

Money drives everything in private equity—it defines what PE firms are and what they pursue. Because of that, they excel at two things: buying companies and exiting them. To succeed on the other side of the table, you must become an expert at understanding both.

You don't need to be a PE professional, but you do need a deep grasp of what happens between the buy and the sell. Take your existing skills in investing or running a business and layer on a clear understanding of how PE firms structure deals, create value, and plan their exits. Only then can you influence outcomes, make an impact, and truly succeed in the PE environment.

Excessive Cost-Cutting And Forgetting The Customer

The 6.6-billion-dollar Toys "R" Us buyout was a high-profile bet that debt-fueled scale would outmuscle Amazon and Walmart, only to collapse under its own leverage before it could adapt to marketplace changes. In 2005, Bain Capital, KKR, and Vornado Realty Trust took Toys "R" Us private for $6.6 billion, loading the once-dominant toy maker with more than $5 billion in debt and roughly $400 million in annual interest obligations. While the brand still held strong recognition, the capital structure left little room to invest in e-commerce, pricing, or store experience at a time when Amazon, Target, and Walmart were rapidly reshaping toy retail.

A failed initial public offering (IPO) attempt in 2010 to 2011 left the company trapped with its LBO-era leverage. In 2017, vendors shortened payment terms ahead of the critical holiday season. Liquidity tightened, pushing Toys "R" Us into Chapter 11. Continuing competitive pressure and eroding supplier confidence forced full US liquidation in 2018. This resulted in approximately 850 stores being shut down and more than 32,000 job losses. The case underscores how in low-margin, fast-changing retail, high financial leverage can starve innovation, magnify downside risk, and turn an iconic brand into a cautionary tale.

The Toys "R" Us story exemplifies a stark reality: one in ten PE-owned companies go into financial restructuring or bankrupt, sometimes one in five for more aggressive firms.

Toys "R" Us became a cautionary tale of the age-old PE playbook: leverage up a company, extract as much cash as possible through real estate deals and cost-cutting, but ultimately lose sight of the consumer walking the aisles and shopping the store. Without the ability to outmaneuver competitors like Walmart, Target, and Amazon, the company couldn't invest adequately in innovation, shelf sets, store layout, and e-commerce to create a compelling consumer experience.

What consumers saw wasn't a thoughtfully designed retail destination—it was a warehouse stuffed with goods. Once that perception takes hold, it creates a vicious cycle. The investments needed to rebuild the experience cost more than the initial investment would have, but the company's leverage prevents those investments from happening. Toys "R" Us lost the consumer plot while chasing the financial leveraging plot and eventually went bankrupt.

How Private Equity Stacks Up Against Other Alternative Investments

Private equity does not operate in isolation. For institutional and individual investors allocating capital, it competes directly with other alternative asset classes: venture capital, hedge funds, infrastructure, and real assets. Each offers a distinct profile in terms of risk, return, and liquidity, and private equity's appeal is best understood when viewed against this broader landscape.

Venture Capital occupies the highest-risk corner of the spectrum. Venture investors back early-stage companies with limited or no cash flow, relying on the outsized success of a few winners to offset a large number of failures. The payoff can be extraordinary, but it is binary: either a company becomes a "unicorn," or it disappears. Unlike private equity, which leans on leverage and operational discipline, venture investing is primarily about growth potential and founder vision. For limited partners, the core question is risk appetite. If private equity resembles a middle-distance race, venture capital is a well-thought-through high-stakes lottery.

Hedge Funds operate under a very different model. They trade in liquid securities and often use leverage, derivatives, or complex strategies to generate returns. Unlike private equity, hedge funds offer periodic liquidity, typically quarterly or annually, and investors can redeem their capital without waiting a decade. Yet that liquidity comes at a cost: over the past decade, hedge fund performance has compressed, with many managers struggling to consistently outperform benchmarks after fees. By contrast, private equity sacrifices liquidity but offers more control over outcomes, since firms take direct ownership of businesses rather than trading around them.

Infrastructure and Real Assets sit at the other end of the continuum. Investments in toll roads, airports, utilities, renewable energy, and pipelines generate stable, long-duration cash flows. Returns are generally lower than those targeted by private equity but are far more predictable, and the underlying assets often serve as an inflation hedge. For pensions and insurers with long-term liabilities, these assets are a natural fit. The tradeoff is less upside, but also far less operational and execution risk.

In this context, private equity represents a *hybrid between growth and income.* It offers the potential for higher returns than infrastructure or hedge funds, while providing more control and maturity than venture capital. Yet it also carries risks that are frequently underappreciated, particularly around liquidity, transparency, and concentration. Unlike hedge funds, capital cannot simply be redeemed. Unlike infrastructure, cash flow is not guaranteed. And unlike venture capital, a fund may hold only ten to fifteen concentrated positions, where mistakes are harder to offset. That combination of leverage, active ownership, and concentrated bets is what makes private equity unique and why investors must carefully consider where it fits within a diversified alternatives portfolio.

Alternatives Landscape Comparison

Asset Class	Typical Returns	Risk Profile	Liquidity	Control / Influence	Time Horizon
Private Equity	Net IRR ~10%–15% (top funds higher)	Moderate to high; leverage and concentration	Locked for 7–10 years	Direct ownership and operational control	10+ years (frequently longer)
Venture Capital	Highly variable; few "home runs" drive returns	Very high; early-stage failure rates common	Locked for 10+ years	Minority stakes; influence varies by founder	10+ years
Hedge Funds	Single digits to low teens; compressed vs. benchmarks	Moderate; market/strategy risk, less control	Quarterly or annual redemption windows	No control; trading strategies in public markets	Short-term to multi-year
Infrastructure & Real Assets	Mid to high single digits; stable with inflation linkage	Low to moderate; regulatory/political risks	Long-term; some assets semi-liquid	Moderate; long-term contracts, regulation-driven	10–20+ years

Fundraising Mechanics And Investor (LP) Relationships

At the heart of private equity isn't just deal-making, it's fundraising. Every few years, PE firms (general partners—GPs) return to their investors (limited partners—LPs): pension funds, sovereign wealth funds, insurance companies, family offices, and endowments to pitch the next fund. The dance is predictable: glossy pitch decks, promises of "alpha" (returns higher than the public markets for a stated level of risk), and carefully curated track records. But beneath the surface lies a tension between LPs and GPs—LPs want transparency, steady returns, and lower fees; GPs want long lock-up periods, carried interest, and the flexibility to invest on their own terms. This structural push-and-pull shapes how aggressively PE firms pursue deals and how they report their outcomes.

Fundraising isn't just a back-office exercise; it directly drives strategy. A fund raised from risk-tolerant LPs may lean heavily into distressed assets or emerging markets. A fund backed by conservative institutions may chase safer rollups in healthcare or business services. LP appetite can determine sector exposure, leverage levels, and even the length of holding periods. Increasingly, LPs demand co-investment rights, giving them the ability to put capital directly into specific deals alongside the PE firm, often at lower fees. This democratizes some upside but can dilute the GP's control and economics.

Another shift is the rise of **secondary markets and continuation funds**. When traditional exits aren't available, GPs now ask LPs for permission to "roll over" assets into new vehicles, effectively extending ownership. For LPs, this means either committing fresh capital or being forced to sell at a discount. For GPs, it's a way to keep assets on the books and keep management fees flowing. It's a reminder that fundraising is not just about new commitments; it's about constant negotiation over liquidity, alignment, and trust.

KEY CHAPTER TAKEAWAYS

1. Two Numbers Rule Everything
- EBITDA and cash flow dominate every PE conversation.
- Culture, brand, and innovation only matter when they move those numbers.

2. Fundraising Is the Engine
- Successful exits fuel strong fundraising, which funds the next cycle.
- Without attractive reported returns, the machine stalls.

3. The Clock Always Ticks
- Holding periods average three to seven years, but pressure starts in months.
- Long-term plays rarely survive if they don't align with fund timelines.

4. Strategy Must Translate into Measurable Value
- Vision only works if it connects to EBITDA and cash-flow growth.
- Start with the numbers, then wrap strategy around them.

5. The Ruthless Simplicity of the Model
- Buy low, improve or cut, exit high—that's the formula.
- Everything else is noise unless it supports that arc.

6. Survival Depends on Discipline
- Firms live or die by fundraising and by net returns after fees.
- That's why speed, leverage, and cost management feel non-negotiable.

7. It's a Marathon Run as a Series of Sprints
- CEOs describe portfolio life as "ninety-day races, repeated for years."
- Miss two quarters, and pressure intensifies dramatically.

8. PE's Role in Capitalism
- PE reallocates capital and labor to more efficient uses.
- Its impact isn't inherently good or bad—it depends on execution.

9. Competing Within the Alternatives Landscape
- PE sits between venture (high risk) and infrastructure (low risk).
- Its mix of control, concentration, and leverage makes it unique.

10. To Win, Master Both Sides of the Equation
- Success comes from understanding how PE buys and how it sells.
- Executives who align with that cycle become indispensable.

You now understand what PE firms do and what they care about. Next, I will dissect how deals are actually structured and what cracks them apart before they even close.

CHAPTER 2

The Anatomy of a PE Deal (And Where It Can Fall Apart)

Buying and selling companies is the engine of private equity. But in deals, paper wins and reality often loses. Even the cleanest-looking transactions can unravel after closing, undone by hidden risks. Many due-diligence misses trace back to outdated systems, compliance gaps, or bad data dressed up as aggressive adjustments. If you buy the story and miss the skeletons, you're left holding a time bomb.

In this chapter, I will go through how PE firms actually do deals and what are the things that can make a deal fall apart before the paper is even signed.

Regulatory Risks That Destroy Value Overnight

It's imperative that you go beyond the surface with due diligence. You need to stress-test systems, assumptions, and unseen liabilities.

I've seen deals implode due to hidden due-diligence issues that were brushed aside in the past. Take a global consumer products company where more than 40% of the profits were coming from one country in Asia that had massive tariff risk. This was a highly risky situation where that EBITDA and cash flow from that business could collapse quickly based on regulatory issues.

I saw a separate deal unwind because of regulatory issues. The deal assumed the regulatory environment would stay unchanged— a convenient but risky bet. A quick look back showed that just five or six years earlier, the tax rules on moving goods in and out of the country had been very different and could easily revert back in current times. That's exactly what happened a year or two after signing, wiping out 15%–20% of the company's value.

The Technology Trap: When Legacy Systems Become Capital Drains

A great deck doesn't guarantee a great deal. Another area where PE deals can fall apart before they're even signed is legacy systems.

Post-close integration costs often balloon because of outdated infrastructure that wasn't flagged early, especially information technology (IT) systems and prolonged periods of delayed or reduced capital expenditures (CapEx). It's imperative that PE firms looking at new deals get behind the actual capabilities that exist now, along with the historical CapEx that's been invested in machinery, equipment, production, and supply chain over the last five-plus years. If systems don't scale or communicate, value evaporates quickly through delays, friction, and unforeseen additional CapEx costs that emerge after the due-diligence phase.

This requires deep IT due diligence early, not just as a checkbox. It also requires deep CapEx assessment of machinery, equipment, production, and supply chain capabilities. I experienced this first-hand where an operator failed to flag outdated systems, leading to massive post-close integration costs. We faced more than $5 million in unforeseen IT costs just to bring systems up to date. The initial due diligence indicated that IT systems could be integrated and scaled. The reality was that systems had to be completely revamped before scalability could happen and before they could be used for bolt-on M&A (acquiring smaller companies in similar businesses). Getting IT scalable is crucial so that future acquisitions can happen.

To be successful during the operating period of a portfolio company, you need systems that work both internally—driving all transactions of the company—and externally for e-commerce that's scalable, updatable, and modernized.

In one deal I worked on, the tech environment was brushed over in the due-diligence phase, assuming it was adequate. In reality, it was so old and unmodernized, including an AS/400 system, that it needed to be upgraded just to prevent internal tech failures. That required multi-million dollars of investment. Beyond that, there were a plethora of issues. Each brand had its own website thrown together using older technology. All of that had to be upgraded into one seamless Shopify-type e-commerce experience across the company, which required significant additional investment. Then the company got ready to merge or acquire another large business. All of those investments became even more critical because to integrate the new business and scale up to the combined size, 50% to 60% larger than the original business, the tech had to be modern and scalable.

More extensive due diligence would have identified those hidden costs upfront, and they could have been built into the plan as CapEx and operating expenses. Digital gaps become capital losses fast.

When Market Drift Destroys Beloved Brands

Another critical area that demands attention is understanding consumer and customer trends—what I call market drift. Even the most beloved brands can crash when private equity chases growth over customer connection, creating consumer blind spots that prove fatal.

It's important to understand category growth rates in the territories where the company operates. But you can't stop there. You must also look at trends and what might happen in the future—not just with the category, but with the actual brands and customers you're dealing with. The consumer landscape can shift beneath your feet, and if you're not watching, you'll miss the warning signs.

Misaligned Strategies
And A Rushed Exit

The rise and fall of Seraphine, once a darling of British retail, offers a vivid lesson in how misjudged strategy and impatience for an exit can destroy value. Founded in 2002 by Cécile Reinaud, Seraphine built a loyal global following for premium maternity wear—with celebrity and even royal endorsements that cemented its brand prestige. When Mayfair Equity Partners acquired the company in December 2020 for roughly £50 million, Seraphine was profitable, growing steadily, and well positioned to benefit from its strong e-commerce presence during the pandemic.

Within less than two years, Mayfair pushed Seraphine into a London IPO at a valuation approaching £150 million. The listing, launched in July 2021, was touted as a validation of the brand's global appeal. But beneath the surface, the move exposed the company to the full volatility of public markets before it had scaled sufficiently to handle them. Operational growing pains, supply chain cost inflation, and rising digital marketing expenses quickly eroded margins. As sales lagged and costs rose, confidence in management's forecasts collapsed.

The founder—who had stepped away after the buyout—later described the company's decline as "heartbreaking," noting that the brand she built had lost its way. Mayfair's post-acquisition strategy involved rebranding initiatives and product changes that critics said diluted Seraphine's original identity. Combined with an ill-timed float during a period of tightening consumer spending, the result was disastrous. The share price plunged more than 90% within a year, and by early 2023, Mayfair was forced to buy back the company through a take-private deal valued at only £15 million, a fraction of its IPO valuation.

The reprieve proved short-lived. Despite efforts to restructure, Seraphine couldn't recover from falling revenues and loss of consumer trust. In July 2025, the company entered administration, leading to widespread job losses. Its once-coveted brand and intellectual property were sold to Next plc for just £600,000, marking a near-total erosion of shareholder value.

Seraphine's collapse underscores how private equity discipline can backfire when short-term exit pressures overshadow long-term brand stewardship. The brand's undoing was not only about timing—it was about misalignment. In the rush to monetize momentum, Mayfair underestimated the fragility of a premium niche brand suddenly thrust into the unforgiving glare of the public market. It stands as a stark reminder that speed without strategic coherence can destroy more than it creates.

How Private Equity Firms Execute A Deal (In Layman's Terms)

Once a private equity firm finds a company it wants to buy, the process becomes a carefully orchestrated project that moves through several stages. Think of it as a relay race: the deal team passes the baton between valuation, due diligence, negotiations, legal documents, financing, and finally closing. Each step is designed to lower the risk of surprises and ensure the firm pays the right price while setting the company up for success under new ownership.

Internal Approval and Advisors—The first step is alignment inside the firm. The investment team brings the deal to their Investment Committee, presenting the business case, the risks, and how they plan to make money from the deal. If approved, the firm mobilizes a small army of outside advisors. These include accountants to verify the company's true earnings, strategy consultants to test whether the market is growing or shrinking, lawyers to dig into contracts and liabilities, IT specialists to review systems, HR experts to examine pensions and retention, and tax advisors to optimize the structure. Even insurance brokers get involved, helping arrange "reps and warranties insurance" that protects the buyer if the seller misrepresented the business.

Valuation and Financing—At the same time, the firm works on valuation and financing. While multiple methods exist, private equity focuses heavily on two tools: comparable EBITDA multiples and discounted cash flow (DCF). Comparable multiples look at how similar companies are valued in public markets or recent transactions, giving a quick benchmark. The DCF, by contrast, projects all future cash flows of the business and discounts them back to today to arrive at an intrinsic value. Layered on top of these methods is the leveraged buyout (LBO) model, which tests how much debt the company can safely carry and what kind of investor returns are achievable under different scenarios. Together, these methods define the price range the firm is willing to pay.

Letter of Intent and Exclusivity—Once comfortable with the terms of the deal, the firm issues a letter of intent (LOI). This is not the final contract but a document that spells out the price range, deal structure, and timeline, and usually locks in a period of exclusivity. That exclusivity is important—it allows the buyer to spend heavily on diligence without worrying another bidder will swoop in at the last minute.

Confirmatory Due Diligence—With exclusivity secured, the confirmatory due-diligence phase begins. Here is where all the advisors dive deep:

- Financial diligence normalizes reported earnings, adjusts for one-time items, and checks if profits truly convert to cash.
- Commercial diligence tests the strength of the market, customer loyalty, and pricing power.
- Legal diligence scans for risks hidden in contracts, litigation, or compliance.

- Tax, IT, HR, and environmental reviews surface issues and costs that might not show up on the income statement.

Each red flag is logged, priced, and negotiated. If the company's reported earnings were overly generous, the purchase price comes down. If environmental liabilities or cyber weaknesses are uncovered, they may require escrows, insurance, or contractual fixes.

Financing and Negotiating the Purchase Agreement— Meanwhile, financing is locked in. Banks or private credit funds provide commitment letters guaranteeing debt financing, while the private equity firm finalizes its own equity commitments. The goal is to walk into contract signing with certainty of funds, giving the seller confidence the deal will close.

The heart of the negotiation is the purchase agreement, a lengthy legal contract that sets the rules of the transaction. This covers price mechanics (whether the price will be adjusted after closing for working capital or locked at a fixed date), the representations and warranties the seller is making, and the remedies if something proves false. Increasingly, insurance policies backstop these promises, shifting risk from buyer and seller to the insurer. The agreement also spells out covenants—what the seller can and cannot do between signing and closing—and conditions that must be satisfied before closing, such as antitrust or regulatory approvals.

Preparation for Ownership—If the business is being carved out of a larger company, additional agreements like transition services agreements (TSAs) are negotiated. These let the seller keep providing IT systems, payroll, or back-office support for a period until the new owner can manage the company on its own.

In parallel, the private equity firm begins preparing for ownership. A hundred-day plan is drafted before closing, detailing how to stabilize the company, keep key employees, communicate with customers and suppliers, and begin the path to growth. This plan is as critical as the deal itself—without it, value creation can quickly stall.

Closing and Post-Close—Finally, the closing arrives. Funds are wired according to a detailed funds flow memo, the seller hands over the keys, and the private equity firm steps in as the new owner. Post-closing, there are still tasks to resolve: finalizing working capital adjustments, enforcing transition agreements, and ensuring all systems and governance are in place. But by this point, the hard work of diligence and negotiation pays off—the baton is passed from deal execution to portfolio management.

KEY CHAPTER TAKEAWAYS

1. Paper Wins, Reality Breaks
- A deal may look flawless on paper but still collapse after closing.
- Hidden risks—regulatory, operational, or technological—often surface only once the ink is dry.

2. Due Diligence Must Go Beyond the Obvious
- Checking the numbers isn't enough—you must stress-test assumptions, systems, and liabilities.
- Many deal failures stem from brushing aside uncomfortable findings rather than confronting them early.

3. Regulatory Risks Can Kill Overnight
- Profits concentrated in a single market or reliant on favorable rules are fragile.
- A sudden tariff, tax, or compliance shift can erase 15%–20% of value almost instantly.

4. Legacy Systems Are Capital Traps
- Outdated IT and neglected CapEx often balloon into multimillion-dollar surprises post-close.
- Tech diligence must be deep, not a checkbox—scalable systems are critical for M&A bolt-ons and growth.

5. Market Drift Is Silent but Deadly
- Beloved brands can fade fast if consumer shifts aren't tracked.
- Category trends and brand positioning must be analyzed dynamically, not just historically.

6. Speed Without Wisdom Destroys Value
- Rushed exits and misaligned strategies—like Seraphine's IPO—can unravel hard-won gains.
- A premature push to cash out often sacrifices brand equity, jobs, and long-term value.

7. Every Deal Is a Relay Race
- Buying a company involves multiple handoffs: valuation → diligence → negotiation → financing → closing.
- Each stage is designed to catch risks and reduce surprises, but weak links can sink the deal.

8. Valuation Is Both Science and Art
- PE firms lean heavily on comparable EBITDA multiples, DCF models, and LBO analysis.
- These tools set the price range, but their accuracy depends on realistic assumptions about earnings and cash flow.

9. The Hundred-Day Plan Is Non-Negotiable
- Preparation for ownership begins before closing.
- Without a disciplined first hundred-day plan to stabilize, retain talent, and reassure customers, value creation stalls.

10. Ask the Only Question That Matters
- Are we interrogating the story behind the numbers, or just falling in love with projections?
- Deals break not on term sheets but on what was missed in diligence and ignored in preparation.

Now that you know the game PE firms are playing, it's time to follow the moves from deal flow to exit. In the next chapter, you'll see how strategy bends to fit the clock and why exit timing drives everything.

CHAPTER 3

Deal Flow to Exit—What Really Drives PE Strategy

I watched a deal come together not because of a perfect fit but because it aligned with the PE firm's exit model. I realized the real goal wasn't operational excellence; it was selling at a higher multiple as quickly as possible.

When you engage with a PE firm—whether as a seller or an executive joining a portfolio company—they'll often say they're long-term investors and that exit timing simply depends on how things evolve. They'll claim they're happy to hold as long as it takes.

That's not the whole truth.

In private equity, time is money—and one of the biggest drivers of IRR (internal rate of return—annualized investment return percentage). Exit timing is everything. Once a firm acquires a company, the clock starts ticking and the pressure is on to exit as quickly and profitably as possible.

Two factors fundamentally distinguish a PE-owned company from a publicly traded one: exit timing and the absence of outside scrutiny. Exit timing is the most critical. The pressure it creates is what truly separates private equity from public ownership. That pressure drives an entirely different culture—one that trades deliberation for speed, favors action over analysis, and seeks rapid value creation through cost cuts, asset sales, and real estate moves.

In this chapter, you'll learn how PE strategy is built by reverse-engineering from the exit backward—and why seeing through that lens is essential to making the right moves at every stage. Remember what we talked about in chapter one: fundraising and reported portfolio returns are the two most important things that drive private equity firms. Once you internalize that, you see why exit timing is so critical—it directly drives reported fund returns, company by company. The exit determines everything even before the deal closes.

Financial Engineering Over Operational Excellence

PE firms rarely give much weight to revenue synergies or organic growth in their forecasts. Most of the value in their buy-and-exit strategy comes from financial leverage, cost reduction, and operational improvements that drive cash flow and EBITDA.

I once worked on a deal that was green lit not for its operational fit but because it matched the PE firm's exit math. In other words, when PE firms think they can exit at a good time, at a good return, they don't necessarily need to have some elaborate, great marketing or operational strategy. In fact, a deal driven by financial engineering and exit timing is much preferred to a deal driven by operational or marketing strategies. It's less risky.

The Tyranny Of The Ticking Clock

The way to think about it is that you need to work backward from the finish line. Even while they are working on buying a company, PE firms shape their strategy around exit timing, target buyers, and valuation multiples—well before operational plans take form. The financial model and exit plan matter more than the marketing, operations, or performance plans of the business.

If you build a business that's great to run but hard to sell, you may never get full credit or even get acquired at all. As a portfolio executive leader, you may never get the exit you want. In fact, you may get replaced and someone else will do the exit for you.

When you are part of a PE deal, start with the end in mind, because the timeline is tighter than most realize. The clock is king. Most PE funds operate on a three-to-seven-year timeline, and that ticking clock shapes every choice. Reverse-engineer every strategic choice from the most likely exit scenario. You also need to have multiple exit scenarios. You might carry out a trade sale, sell to another private equity firm, sell to a continuation fund (see detailed explanation later), or execute an IPO. It's important to consider multiple exit strategies and determine how you're going to make the exit happen within the time needed to get a good return.

Every successful operator can be undervalued if they don't hit that exit window. You can deliver great customer metrics and operational turnarounds, but if cash flow and EBITDA aren't growing according to forecast (especially toward that exit), you'll be unsuccessful. If you don't show progress fast enough, you may be sidelined or replaced even if your long-term play is solid. Align your pacing to the fund's timeline and make time your strategic ally.

I know a specific case where an operator delivered outstanding results—reversing market share declines, transforming customer relationships, and building a world-class supply chain that stripped out major costs. But external shocks—Covid disruptions, trade pressures, and tariff changes—shifted the timeline. The turnaround no longer fit the PE firm's clock. They exited, and in the end, no value was realized for the firm or the leadership team.

Speed As Competitive Advantage

Speed isn't optional—it's the currency of private equity. The focus must stay fixed on the exit: its timing, its pathway, and the flexibility to pursue multiple strategies to get there.

Because of the pressure that exit timing brings, everything must be done quicker and faster. If there's a leadership change needed on the team, do it immediately. If there are overhead cost cuts to make, execute them in sixty to ninety days rather than the six months or year a public company might take. If you have an asset that is not strategic, can it be sold in four months instead of twelve? Everything is based on speed because everything traces back to the exit timeline. Any delay in operational plans or business success delays the exit plan and reduces the overall deal return.

The Engineered Flip Playbook

Some of the best exits are engineered flips, not operational masterpieces. A significant percentage of PE deals are flips and engineered exit strategies rather than actual operational transformations.

The magic happens when you buy a company facing market headwinds, acquire it at a below-average multiple, and let the math work in your favor. You lever it up—raising debt from a typical public-company level of 20%–25% to around 50% of the balance sheet—and drive modest cost savings in overhead and supply chain while holding market share. Then, as the economy strengthens and industry multiples rise, timing does the rest. The combination of leverage, cost discipline, and market recovery delivers an excellent exit and strong returns—all within a familiar playbook built on timing.

If you're looking for long-term alignment or continuity, PE may frustrate you. If you want to work in the PE-portfolio company environment, the best way to look at it is as multiple opportunities over a ten-year period, rather than one or two. Some PE deals might go longer than you think, but remember, with the exit timeline being the most important thing, don't be afraid to get in in the middle or the back end of a deal. In fact, in many cases that is a lower-risk strategy.

Make things happen quickly. Move twice as fast as you would in a public-company environment. Get things done and then move on to the next deal. There's nothing wrong with that approach. If you're someone who's looking to work at the same place for ten-plus years, PE may not be the right fit for you on the operating side of the business.

BUSINESS CASE

A CASE STUDY IN PERFECT TIMING

PetSmart and Chewy, backed by BC Partners, illustrate how timing and structure—not operational brilliance—can deliver staggering private equity returns. This case isn't about synergy;

it's about knowing when to buy, when to hold, and exactly when to let go.

When BC Partners acquired PetSmart in 2015 for $8.7 billion, the company was a mature, store-heavy retailer under pressure from Amazon and the rapid migration of pet owners to online channels. Two years later, sensing both a threat and an opportunity, PetSmart made a bold move—acquiring Chewy for $3.35 billion in 2017, then the largest e-commerce acquisition in history. The young online retailer, founded by Ryan Cohen, was growing exponentially and had cultivated intense customer loyalty through convenience, personalization, and its innovative AutoShip subscription service.

Crucially, BC Partners and PetSmart resisted the temptation to integrate the two businesses. Instead, they allowed Chewy to maintain its own brand, leadership, and culture—a rare act of restraint in private equity. That decision unlocked enormous growth. Chewy's revenues soared from $2.1 billion in 2017 to more than $3.5 billion by 2019, while its customer base nearly doubled. Investors began to view Chewy as a category-defining digital platform rather than a retail offshoot.

Then came the perfectly timed exit. In 2019, BC Partners took Chewy public at a valuation of $8.8 billion, creating nearly $10 billion in paper gains and using the proceeds to significantly deleverage PetSmart's balance sheet. Within a year, Chewy's market capitalization surpassed that of PetSmart's entire acquisition cost, and by 2020, the two entities were fully separated—leaving BC Partners with substantial realized and unrealized gains on both sides of the transaction.

The Chewy deal became a modern private equity masterclass in timing, capital markets arbitrage, and non-integration strategy. BC Partners' success didn't come from reengineering stores or revamping operations—it came from recognizing that the digital tail could wag the brick-and-mortar dog.

In private equity, the best exits aren't always logical—they're opportunistic. When a firm times its exit perfectly and hits the multiple it modeled at entry, the narrative of value creation almost writes itself. As this case shows, a well-timed IPO can vindicate a thesis even more powerfully than operational turn-around ever could. The right deal, at the right moment, forgives almost everything else.

KEY CHAPTER TAKEAWAYS

1. Exit Timing Is Everything
- PE firms may claim to be long-term investors, but the real value driver is when and how they exit.
- The clock starts ticking the moment a deal closes, shaping every decision from strategy to culture.

2. Strategy Works Backward from the Finish Line
- PE doesn't start with operations and build forward—it starts with the exit and works backward.
- Every move—valuation, financing, leadership—aligns with the most likely exit scenario.

3. Fund Returns Depend on Exits
- Reported portfolio returns, the lifeblood of fundraising, come only from realized exits.
- No matter how good operations look on paper, if the exit doesn't happen on time, value isn't captured.

4. Financial Engineering Trumps Operational Genius
- Most deals are structured around leverage, cost control, and exit math, not revenue growth.
- Deals can succeed with minimal change if the timing and financial structuring are right.

5. The Tyranny of the Clock
- PE funds run deals on three-to-seven-year cycles, and executives must match their pace to that timeline.
- Delivering great results outside the exit window won't matter—you may still be replaced.

6. Speed Is the Currency of PE

- Leadership changes, cost cuts, and asset sales happen in months, not years.
- Velocity itself becomes a competitive advantage; delays are fatal to the exit plan.

7. The Engineered Flip Playbook

- Many of the best returns come from timing and leverage, not bold transformations.
- Buying low, levering up, making incremental improvements, and exiting at a higher multiple is a repeatable formula.

8. PetSmart and Chewy: Timing Beats Synergy

- BC Partners turned PetSmart's Chewy acquisition into billions by keeping Chewy independent and flipping it quickly.
- The case proves that perfect timing and structural decisions can outweigh operational integration.

9. Careers Run on Deal Clocks Too

- Executives in PE-backed companies must think in deal cycles, not decades.
- Success comes from making fast, visible progress toward exit value—not from building the perfect long-term company.

10. The Only Question That Matters: Exit Readiness

- At every step, ask: will this decision make the company easier to sell at a higher multiple within the fund's window?
- If the answer is no, the initiative won't survive under private equity ownership.

Now you understand the art of private equity deals and the absolute importance of exit strategy and timing. In the next chapter, we'll uncover how regulation, ESG, and technology shape private equity, whether you plan for them or not. Even the cleanest deal is exposed to forces you can't control. Live and die by what you don't see.

CHAPTER **4**

The Silent Deal Killers—
ESG, Regulation, and Tech

I was once involved in a deal where we greatly underestimated how much a regulatory change would impact the exit value. It was a situation where a flow of goods out of and then back into the major market for the company resulted in lower value-added taxes (VAT). At the time of the deal, regulatory tax authorities looked at that flow as acceptable, and it was expected to continue for a long period of time.

In reality, it stopped soon after the deal closed.

When VAT was applied and the flow of goods stopped, prices rose too high for the market—wiping out 20% of the company's value.

In this chapter, you'll unpack the silent forces reshaping private equity—regulation, ESG mandates, and tech evolution—and how they can either derail your strategy or become a hidden edge.

The most important of these is the regulatory underbelly. One rule change can vaporize millions in value overnight.

Mapping The Regulatory Minefield

Regulation is one of the biggest risks that can crater a deal after it's signed. The reason is twofold. First, a regulatory change can significantly affect your EBITDA and cash flow. Second, regulatory change is the one change that's least within your control. You can actively manage the cost structure of your business by making decisions about how many people to hire and fire, and how you run your manufacturing plants, supply chain, and distribution. But you don't have much power over politicians or regulators who decide to change a certain law or the way that law is applied.

PE deals often rely on specific tax treatments, legal structures, and compliance frameworks. Policy shifts can upend them instantly. One of the biggest examples of this is tariffs. When doing due diligence on a PE deal, you have to understand the regulatory environment and the potential for tariffs to shift up or down. You also need to be able to plan for worst-case scenarios.

When structuring a deal, you can't assume the current regulatory environment will remain unchanged. It's imperative that you think about what kind of regulatory changes can happen, when they can happen, and what the effect will be on the business. Identify any regulatory changes that could occur, map key regulations that currently underpin the business, and track how changes to those regulations translate directly to changes in cash flow and EBITDA.

If you're not watching the legislative horizon, you'll react too late. It is imperative that you build scenario maps for regulatory risk. Get legal advisors involved early to map revenues and cash flows at risk based on potential regulatory changes. When that rule change hits, there's no time to scramble; the damage is already done.

You have to take regulatory risk as a major risk and get underneath it. You have to look through the history of the company at what regulatory risks have popped up in the past. You need to do a significant amount of brainstorming about what is currently being discussed that could turn into regulation, or what isn't even being discussed but could still affect your business in the future.

Reading The Legislative Tea Leaves

In your major markets, analyze what type of legislation potentially could become reality, not just what's already in action or heading to bill but what could emerge in the future. One effective approach is to examine patterns from the last ten years. You can also conduct deep dives into how legislative bodies and legislators discuss items, even before they become law.

Being prepared for regulatory shifts is critical. You must understand how potential changes could affect your business and plan for worst-case outcomes. That means developing scenario maps for regulatory risk—linking each scenario to the revenues and cash flows most exposed to those changes.

Smart firms focus not only on the deal but on the playing field itself. You need to map the regulatory terrain, anticipate potential shifts, and develop a deep understanding of the landscape.

ESG As A Profit Driver, Not Theater

Now let's examine ESG (environmental, social, and governance). Public companies have significant programs around ESG because it's required by shareowners and politicians. These external forces are less for privately owned companies. In private equity, ESG initiatives only gain traction when they tie directly to EBITDA and cash flow. This isn't about doing good for the sake of it; it's about initiatives that directly impact your bottom line.

In private equity, ESG isn't pursued for moral reasons or as a standalone program—it must drive cash flow and EBITDA. The key connection is when ESG initiatives are genuinely valued by consumers and customers. ESG makes sense in the PE environment when it increases sales, strengthens partnerships, and enhances the brand's commercial value.

You don't want to look at ESG as compliance theater. You want to ask the right questions. How can I get financial leverage out of this? How can I actually create value and measure it as a financial metric rather than just as an ESG program? The way to do that is to connect with your customers and consumers and see how it can drive value with them rather than just become a corporate exercise.

ESG THAT PAID OFF

One of the earliest and most visible examples of ESG in practice within private equity came from KKR. In 2008, the firm launched its Green Portfolio Program (GPP) in partnership with the Environmental Defense Fund (EDF). The initiative wasn't built on moral grandstanding—it was designed around measurable EBITDA impact. KKR reframed sustainability as operational excellence, not philanthropy. Portfolio companies were guided to cut energy use, reduce waste, and improve supply chain efficiency—all tracked in financial terms rather than PR metrics.

Over its first few years, the program delivered substantial results. By 2014, KKR reported that across more than twenty-five participating portfolio companies, the GPP had avoided over 2.3 million metric tons of greenhouse gas emissions, eliminated 27 million cubic meters of water waste, and achieved $1.2 billion in cumulative financial benefits through cost reductions and efficiency gains. Companies like U.S. Foodservice (now US Foods), Dollar General, and First Data were cited as early participants that found direct value from reducing energy intensity and improving logistics. These operational savings flowed straight to the bottom line—providing a blueprint for ESG-driven value creation that was both scalable and repeatable.

The program's influence extended beyond cost-cutting. KKR began linking management incentive plans in certain deals to sustainability KPIs (key performance indicators, or metrics), embedding ESG metrics into how executives were compensated and how success was measured. The firm later expanded this ethos into its Responsible Investment Policy and Sustainability Expert Advisory Council, showing that structured ESG integration could coexist with—and even enhance—traditional private equity rigor. While not every initiative produced measurable gains, the cultural signal was powerful: ESG could be a driver of competitiveness, not a distraction from it.

The bottom line: in private equity, ESG is rarely about virtue—it's about value. When environmental and social initiatives deliver tangible cash-flow improvements or reduce exit risk, they become part of the investment playbook. When they don't, they quickly regress to box-checking. For portfolio executives and sellers alike, the takeaway is clear: understanding how ESG initiatives map to valuation levers can mean the difference between an average exit and a great one. KKR's Green Portfolio Program proved that the most successful ESG efforts speak the language of returns, not rhetoric.

The Tech Multiplier Effect

The last silent killer of deals is the tech multiplier, and this is critical. Digital fluency is now table stakes, as well as a differentiator. It means that you have to get the IT part of the business right. It's a multiplier effect. It's not something that's just necessary to run the business.

There are two key pieces of this. First, you want your IT systems that run the core order to cash cycle (order taking, supply chain, production, account receivables and payables) to be scalable, modern, and easily updated. Second, you want your e-commerce platforms to be customer centric, easy to use, modern, and scalable. That's required for future growth and for M&A activity.

So it's something that you must get right.

Tech upgrades often unlock scale, margin expansion, and smoother exits, and PE firms are underwriting them in deal models. It's critical to secure the right investments upfront, structuring the deal economics to modernize and scale IT systems, and to upgrade e-commerce capabilities in parallel.

Make sure you audit and roadmap your tech stack before due diligence, not during it.

DEEP DIVE

ESG AND STAKEHOLDER CAPITALISM

ESG (environmental, social, and governance) is one of the buzziest topics in private equity today, but it's also one of the most misunderstood. Most PE firms don't prioritize ESG because of a moral imperative. They prioritize it when it ties directly to EBITDA or exit valuation. If a sustainability initiative cuts costs, drives revenue, or helps with a higher multiple at exit, it moves to the top of the list. If not, it usually gets lip service in an annual report and little else.

That doesn't mean ESG is irrelevant. Increasingly, LPs are pushing firms to adopt ESG frameworks, not just because they believe in the cause, but because they see reputational and financial risk if it's ignored. European investors especially are demanding stricter disclosure and measurable improvements in portfolio companies. US firms are responding more slowly, but even here, diversity metrics, carbon footprint reporting, and employee engagement scores are becoming part of diligence checklists and quarterly board decks.

The real driver, though, is exit value. Strategic buyers and public markets increasingly pay a premium for companies with strong ESG credentials, particularly around sustainability and governance. A company that can show lower energy costs, cleaner supply chains, or a diverse and stable workforce often attracts a wider pool of bidders and achieves a better multiple. For PE firms, this isn't about virtue; it's about economics.

There's also a growing risk management angle. Companies without ESG policies face higher regulatory risk, reputational blowups, or even customer backlash. A PE-owned consumer business that gets caught up in a labor scandal or receives an environmental fine can see enterprise value affected overnight. That's why even skeptical GPs are paying more attention: ignoring ESG has become too dangerous.

TECH AS THE NEW PE BATTLEGROUND

For decades, value creation in private equity was shorthand for cost-cutting and financial engineering. But in today's deal landscape, technology is also a decisive battleground. Digital transformation—cloud migration, ERP upgrades, data analytics, and increasingly AI—can determine whether a portfolio company thrives or gets left behind. Yet many PE firms lag in truly embedding technology as a core lever. Too often, IT investments are treated as compliance costs rather than strategic growth drivers.

Smart PE firms now bring in "operating partners" with tech backgrounds, embedding them during diligence to spot hidden risks and opportunities. Cybersecurity, for example, has become a due-diligence landmine; a single overlooked vulnerability can vaporize millions in enterprise value. At the same time, tech can accelerate top-line growth—whether through e-commerce expansion, digital customer engagement, or automation of back-office functions. The firms that understand this create value beyond mere margin expansion; they future-proof companies.

But technology also raises the bar for execution. Portfolio companies that fail to modernize often find themselves at a competitive disadvantage, dragging down exit multiples. Deal models that assume "quick IT upgrades" often underestimate the cost, time, and cultural disruption required. In fact, failed digital transformations are becoming a silent deal killer, just as deadly as leverage missteps or regulatory surprises. For sellers and managers, the lesson is clear: if your tech stack is outdated, a PE buyer will either price that risk in—or exploit it as part of the value-creation plan.

KEY CHAPTER TAKEAWAYS

1. Regulation Can Erase Value Overnight
- A single rule change—tariffs, taxes, or compliance shifts—can vaporize 10%–20% of a company's value.
- Unlike costs you control internally, regulatory risks sit outside your influence.

2. Map the Regulatory Minefield Early
- Don't assume today's rules will hold. Study past shifts, pending legislation, and political signals.
- Build scenario maps linking potential regulatory changes directly to EBITDA and cash flow.

3. Plan for Worst-Case Scenarios
- If you're only modeling "business as usual," you're already behind.
- Stress-test valuations with downside cases where tariffs rise, tax rules flip, or compliance costs surge.

4. ESG Matters—But Only When It Pays
- In PE, ESG succeeds when it drives EBITDA, not when it's a feel-good program.
- Sustainability tied to cost savings, brand preference, or customer contracts earns real traction.

5. LPs (Investors) Are Pushing ESG Harder
- Institutional investors, especially in Europe, now demand measurable ESG progress.
- Strong ESG credentials can expand the buyer pool and lift exit multiples.

6. KKR's Green Portfolio Example

- ESG worked when KKR tied environmental initiatives to cost reduction and operating performance.
- Hundreds of millions in savings proved ESG can be an EBITDA lever, not just compliance theater.

7. Tech Is Now a Valuation Multiplier

- Outdated IT isn't just a headache—it kills scalability, margin expansion, and exit value.
- Modern, cloud-based, integrated systems make M&A integration and e-commerce growth possible.

8. Diligence Must Go Beyond Surface-Level Tech Checks

- Many deals underestimate the cost, time, and disruption of IT upgrades.
- Cybersecurity, e-commerce, and ERP (Enterprise Resource Planning) systems must be audited deeply before close, not after.

9. Tech Partners Are the New Operating Partners

- Forward-thinking firms embed tech-savvy advisors during diligence to spot hidden risks and upside.
- Digital fluency has become a decisive battleground for PE success.

10. Silent Killers Are Also Hidden Levers

- Regulation, ESG, and tech can derail deals—or become competitive advantages if tackled early.
- Smart operators frame them as value drivers in diligence, not compliance costs to deal with later.

In this chapter you learned that hidden forces shift the ground beneath every deal, but not all risk is external. Next, we'll examine what happens when private equity promises returns it can't always deliver, and how to read the real scorecard.

CHAPTER **5**

The Top Quartile Illusion— Understanding Private Equity Returns

I believed in the top-quartile myth until I helped model returns and saw how fees, capital drag, and leverage distorted the picture (capital drag is the reduction in investor returns caused by the time lag between when capital is committed and when it's actually deployed).

Private equity fund returns resemble those of active mutual funds and ETFs (exchange traded funds): most don't beat the market. The top funds perform well, but that's no different from other asset classes. Although private equity is often perceived as consistently delivering superior returns, the reality is much more complex and nuanced.

Private equity fund returns follow a curve similar to other asset classes, with both high and low performers. In addition, over the last three to five years, private equity has underperformed public-market benchmarks due to rising interest rates and overall market conditions. Over the long term, however, the asset class has delivered slightly better overall returns than comparable public-market indexes.

The future wealth created in private equity will rival that of the public markets—a measure of its enormous potential. The key is understanding how it works and doing your homework. With that knowledge, you can choose the right firms to work for, the right firms to sell to, and the right firms to invest with. Get that right, and your future opportunities—in operating, selling, and investing—expand dramatically.

In this chapter, I'll break down the math behind private equity returns. You'll learn why the glossy internal rates of return (IRR) and public-market equivalent (PME) often hide more than they reveal.

The Top-Quartile Illusion

The first thing to understand is the top-quartile illusion. Significantly more than half of PE funds underperform comparable public markets. Despite the marketing hype, this is similar to other asset classes like active equity and bond mutual funds and ETFs (exchange traded funds). It's important to note that a few PE funds greatly outperform others and do beat the market appreciably. The high performance of these funds skew the total average return north of public markets, with a small positive alpha (excess return versus appropriate benchmark). Over long periods of time, it's very difficult for most PE funds to beat the market (after fees) just like it is in any other actively managed asset class.

There has been extensive academic studies and empirical data analysis of historical private equity returns. Some of it is not as concise and perfect as we would like, but the overall summary is that, on average, private equity has gotten roughly one to two percentage points higher investment returns than comparable public indexes over long periods of time. That obviously comes with a price of dramatically less liquidity, different types of investment risks, and less transparency.

It's crucial to thoroughly understand the actual returns of the firms and funds you intend to invest in. Studies show only a minority of private equity funds beat the S&P 500 over full cycles (10-plus years), especially after fees, cash drag, and leverage distortion. It's critical to dig deeper: understand IRR and returns after fees, capital drag, and the distortions of leverage. If you assume alpha or better-than-market returns without examining structure, you're overpaying for performance.

You need to scrutinize net returns and benchmark to public indexes with full transparency. I've seen modeled PE fund returns firsthand and how reported internal rate of returns mask structural inefficiencies. What sounds elite might just be expensive mediocrity.

Fee Fog: The High Cost Structure Reality

PE firms earn money in multiple ways: management fees, carry interest, dividends, etc. These layers systematically eat returns. There's no doubt that private equity operates with one of the highest cost structures of any managed asset class, driven by the hands-on active management required by the model and the different types of fees that PE firms extract to run the total machine.

Over the long run, PE portfolio returns generally overcome these extra fees, ending up roughly equal to—or slightly better than—public-market indices. But it's essential to dig deep into the fee structure and demand transparency. Without that clarity, you risk overstating performance since returns can look stronger than they are when all fees aren't fully accounted for.

These fee structures also reduce cash flow at the portfolio-company level and extract value before investors see it. PE remains an extremely high-cost method of investing and creating value, which explains why the focus on exit timing and returns becomes so intense. It's all a high-pressure loop, and it needs to be that way to overcome the high cost structures inherent in PE firms.

Understanding these cost structures and demanding transparency isn't optional. Even a strong business can yield poor investor returns if fees aren't properly accounted for in your investment thesis.

Transparency Issues: Mapping The True Cost Of Private Equity

Private equity's glossy performance numbers often hide a costly truth. Investors can keep far less than what the funds claim. While private equity firms tout impressive gross returns, these figures often exclude the substantial drag from management fees, carried interest, capital drag, and other charges that investors actually bear. This lack of standardized, transparent reporting means limited partners (investors) may be comparing inflated pre-fee results to net-of-fee public-market benchmarks, creating a misleading sense of outperformance. In addition, both IRR—returns on investor capital as it's deployed and returned—and PME, which compares a fund's performance to public-market benchmarks over time, can be manipulated favorably in several ways. These include using investor capital-backed credit lines, emphasizing deals that have already exited with strong returns, marking up ongoing investments at favorable valuations, and selecting a conveniently favorable public index for comparison.

Investors should map out the full cost structure and understand how potential manipulations can affect reported returns. Break down every layer—management fees, carried interest, and dividends paid from portfolio companies to the PE firm—and understand exactly how the firm calculates IRR and PME. Only by accounting for each component can you build a clear, comparable picture of true net returns after fees.

Once all costs are accounted for, net returns often converge toward—and sometimes can fall below—public equities. Despite the higher illiquidity and complexity of PE investments for investors, the gap between reported and realized performance isn't just an accounting quirk; it's a fundamental risk to capital allocation decisions. It must be understood. The house wins unless you check the spread.

When Institutional Giants Retreat

Even some institutional giants have been pulling back after seeing disappointing PE results. Several of the world's most sophisticated pension and endowment funds are quietly cutting back on private equity exposure. They're not doing this because they can't access deals—they're doing it because years of underperformance and murky fee structures are no longer worth the gamble. Large institutional investors such as Canada's CDPQ, Ontario Municipal Employees Retirement System, Ontario Teachers Pension Plan, and the Texas Teachers Retirement System have scaled back some of their private equity commitments after internal reviews revealed a troubling mix of lower-than-expected returns, opaque cost disclosures, and increasing operational complexity. In many cases, headline performance fell short of public-market benchmarks once full fees and carried interest were factored in. While the lack of real-time valuation transparency hindered effective portfolio risk management, these funds aim to improve liquidity, lower costs, and regain control over governance by reducing direct allocations and favoring public markets or co-investments (direct investments in specific private equity deals rather than funds). The goal is to better align their capital deployment with both fiduciary duty and member expectations.

If the pros are retreating from private equity, individual investors need to reassess their blind spots. Reframe PE as a tool, not as a trophy, and apply institutional-level scrutiny. Don't just say that you need to build X percent of your portfolio in PE and then blindly accept that PE is going to beat the market. You must research the actual returns and ensure that there is real transparency in those returns before you make those decisions.

If you're investing in private equity, treat it as a tool to enhance returns and diversify your portfolio. Like any tool, it requires research and clear understanding. You can't just jump in—you need to know how it works and how it fits into your portfolio.

Scale doesn't guarantee insight—or protection from disappointment. In private equity, size alone doesn't mean a firm will outperform the market. Big firms may have longer histories and deeper track records, but even they run funds that underperform. That's why it's critical to do your homework, understand each firm's and fund's return profile, and look beyond scale to judge performance.

CARRIED INTEREST: THE ENGINE OF PRIVATE EQUITY COMPENSATION

One of the defining features of private equity is the way the people who run the funds (general partners [the PE firm and their employees]) get paid. Beyond management fees, which cover salaries and overhead, the real incentive for private equity professionals (and PE firms) comes from something called carried interest (or simply "carry"). Carried interest is essentially equity—a share of the profits of a fund. It's not a fixed salary, not a bonus tied to short-term results, but equity-based compensation that only pays out if the fund actually creates value for its investors. In this way, carry aligns the interests of the general partners with the limited partners (the pension funds, endowments, institutions, and high-net-worth individuals who provide the capital).

How Carry Works—Typically, carried interest is set at 20% of the profits of a fund, though top-performing firms or specialized strategies can negotiate higher shares. The mechanics start with the investors committing capital—say $1 billion—to a private equity fund. Over the life of the fund, the private equity team invests that capital into companies, improves them, and eventually sells them.

Here's where the details matter. In most cases, investors must be repaid not only their original capital but also a minimum "preferred return" (the hurdle rate, often around 8%) before carry is triggered. This structure is designed to ensure that limited partners earn a baseline return before the general partners share in the profits. Only after that hurdle is cleared does the 20% carry apply. This is the most common approach for large, institutional funds and is often referred to as the "European waterfall."

In other cases—especially with smaller or more GP-friendly funds—the hurdle may be lower, or absent entirely. Some funds also calculate carry on a deal-by-deal basis (the "American waterfall"), allowing managers to collect carry from successful exits even if other investments in the same fund later lose money. To protect investors, these funds usually include clawback provisions, requiring GPs to return excess carry if the fund as a whole underperforms.

The practical outcome is that carry can mean enormous payouts. A successful ten-billion-dollar fund that doubles its money could generate more than a billion dollars in carried interest (or equity gains) for its partners. But the flip side is also true: if the fund underperforms or merely returns investor capital without profits, the managers earn little or no carry at all. That all-or-nothing structure is why carried interest is often described as the equity compensation of private equity—it ties managers' wealth directly to the long-term performance of their fund portfolio.

Why Carry Matters to PE Firms—Carried interest isn't just a perk; it's the foundation of private equity economics. Management fees keep the lights on, but carry is the real wealth generator. It motivates deal teams to think like owners, to take risks, and to focus on value creation rather than short-term financial engineering. For investors, this alignment of interests is central to the appeal of the asset class: if the fund wins, both LPs and GPs win together. If the fund fails, the GPs don't walk away rich.

Carry also explains why private equity attracts entrepreneurial talent. The chance to share directly in the upside of building and selling businesses is a huge draw. In many cases, carried interest payouts have made senior partners of major firms billionaires, while also spreading meaningful wealth to junior partners and rising stars. The structure creates a clear hierarchy and incentive ladder within firms—those who prove themselves and rise into the partnership share directly in the profits.

For most GP structures, the PE firm will keep 40%–50% of the carried interest profits earned and distribute the remaining share to its employees working on the deal. So, carry drives significant profitability for both the PE firm and for its employees associated with the deals.

The Tax Debate—While carried interest is fundamental to private equity, it has long been controversial because of how it is taxed. In most jurisdictions, carried interest is treated as a capital gain rather than ordinary income. That means instead of being taxed at higher income tax rates (as wages or bonuses would be), carry benefits from lower long-term capital gains rates. In the US, this can mean a tax rate of around 20% instead of up to 37% for ordinary income.

Critics argue this is unfair, since private equity professionals are being compensated for their labor and expertise, not for risking their own money. They see carried interest as income in disguise and argue it should be taxed at the same rate as salaries and bonuses. Supporters, however, counter that carry is different: it is only earned when actual investment gains are realized and only if investors make money. In their view, it is genuinely a share of the profits, not just a fee.

The debate has become political. "Closing the carried interest loophole" has been proposed repeatedly in the US Congress, and each time it sparks heated arguments between those who want to raise taxes on private equity professionals and those who warn that doing so could reduce entrepreneurship, investment, and risk-taking. So far, the treatment has remained largely intact, but it continues to be a lightning rod issue whenever tax reform is on the table.

Wrapping Up—Carried interest is the lifeblood of private equity compensation. It ties the success of fund managers directly to the performance of their investors, fuels the industry's culture of ownership, and explains both the enormous wealth it creates and the controversy that surrounds it. Like any equity-based pay, it is simple in principle but powerful in practice. Without carry, private equity would look like just another form of asset management. With it, the incentives are supercharged—rewarding those who can consistently create value and sparking ongoing debate about whether the tax system is too generous to them.

UNDERSTANDING THE DISTRIBUTION OF PRIVATE EQUITY RETURNS

Private equity is often pitched as an asset class that consistently beats the public markets, but the truth is far more complicated. The overall numbers look attractive: across long periods, private equity funds have delivered an average net return of about 12%, compared to around 10% for US public equities. On the surface, that two-percentage-point spread seems like a clear win. But averages hide enormous differences in performance across funds—and it's the distribution that tells the real story.

When we break down the data, a clear pattern emerges: the bottom 65% of private equity funds actually underperform or barely match public equities. Many of these funds generate returns in the 6%–8% range—decent in isolation, but hardly worth the illiquidity, fees, and complexity of private equity compared to simply owning a broad market index. This is the uncomfortable reality for most investors: the majority of private equity funds do not deliver the "alpha" often advertised.

The middle quartile of funds does somewhat better, typically posting returns around 10%–12%. These managers deliver modest outperformance, but the spread over public markets is small—usually just enough to justify the risk for institutions that can lock up capital, but not transformative. These funds show that while private equity can edge out the market, it doesn't always produce blockbuster results.

The real story is in the top quartile of funds, which consistently generate significant excess returns. Here, net IRRs often reach 15%–20% or more, and these winners pull the overall average upward. In fact, without these top performers, the private equity industry's return premium over the public market would all but disappear. The outsized gains of a relatively small group of funds mask the mediocrity of the majority.

Case Study: Blackstone—Blackstone is an example of a firm that has consistently delivered top-quartile performance over multiple cycles. Its Hilton Hotels investment, which turned a near-disastrous pre-crisis buyout into a record-setting exit, is just one example. Across its flagship buyout funds, Blackstone has regularly achieved net returns in the mid-to-high teens, well above public benchmarks. For investors able to secure an allocation, Blackstone exemplifies the kind of consistent top-quartile performance that defines private equity's reputation.

Case Study: CalPERS—Contrast that with the California Public Employees' Retirement System (CalPERS), one of the largest PE investors in the world. Despite its size and access, CalPERS has repeatedly disclosed that much of its PE portfolio has underperformed expectations. Many of the funds it invested in delivered returns barely above—and sometimes below—public equities, especially after fees. The problem wasn't exposure to the asset class, but exposure to too many "average" funds rather than consistent top-quartile performers.

For investors, the lesson is simple but critical: manager selection drives outcomes in private equity more than in almost any other asset class. Unlike public equities, where buying the index guarantees you the market return, in private equity your results depend almost entirely on gaining access to the right managers. Top-tier funds are oversubscribed and selective about their investors, while average funds are far easier to access—which is precisely the problem.

The bottom line is that private equity can indeed outperform public equities, but it doesn't do so evenly across the board. The average looks good because of a small number of exceptional funds. For investors, the challenge is not deciding whether private equity as a whole is attractive—the data says it is—but whether they can realistically access the managers who deliver those top-quartile returns. Without that access, the odds of beating the public market are no better than a coin toss, and often worse.

Approximate Distribution of US Private Equity Fund Returns vs. US Public Equity Markets: Very Long Term (50+ years)

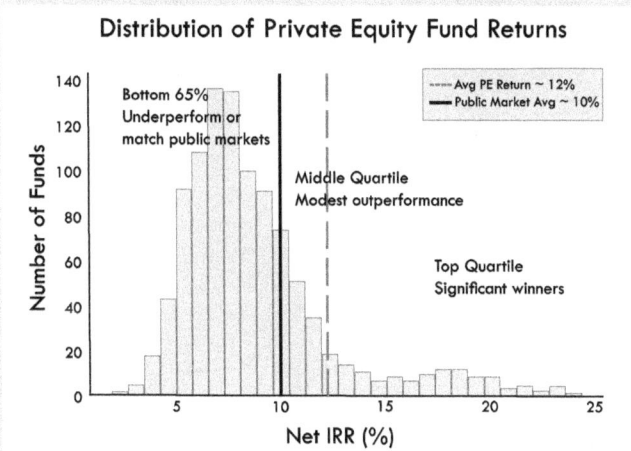

Figure 1: Approximate Distribution of Private Equity Fund Returns

While private equity has historically delivered average net returns of ~12%, compared to ~10% for public markets, the distribution is highly uneven. The bottom ~65% of funds underperform or match public equities. The middle quartile shows modest outperformance, and the top quartile generates significant gains, highlighting the importance of manager selection.

KEY CHAPTER TAKEAWAYS

1. "Top Quartile" Is Mostly Marketing
- Most PE funds don't beat broad public indexes over full cycles.
- A small set of winners pulls up the average and fuels the myth.

2. Net, Not Gross
- Always read net IRR after all fees, carry, and cash drag—not headline gross numbers.
- If you can't reconcile net-of-fee results, you don't know the truth.

3. Fees and Capital Drag Are Gravity
- Management fees, carry, monitoring fees, and capital call timing systematically pull returns down.
- Even strong businesses can yield weak investor outcomes if fee drag isn't modeled.

4. IRR Can Lie (While Being Technically True)
- IRR flatters short holds, leverage, and early partial exits; it's a timing metric, not a wealth metric.
- Cross-check with multiples on invested capital (MOIC) and public-market equivalents (PME).

5. Averages Hide a Lopsided Distribution
- The bottom half (and often more) of funds match or lag public markets.
- The return premium lives on the right side of the tail—which most investors don't access.

6. Access Is the Edge
- Outcomes hinge on manager selection and fund access more than asset-class selection.

- "Getting into" consistently top-tier GPs is the strategy; everything else is beta (volatility risk) with fees.

7. Scale ≠ Skill
- Big brands and large funds still run underperforming fund cycles.
- Judge each fund and fund cycle on its own net record; don't outsource conviction to reputation.

8. Institutions Are Recalibrating—So Should You
- When pensions and endowments dial back PE after fee and return reviews, take the hint.
- Treat private equity investment as a tool, not a trophy allocation; require transparency that you can actually verify.

9. Benchmark Like an Adult
- Compare to the correct public proxy with full-cycle, after-fee data.
- Demand look-through reporting on fees, dividend recaps, and portfolio-company cash extraction.

10. Illiquidity Isn't a Free Lunch
- The "premium" for lockups, opacity, and complexity is earned only if you pick the right managers.
- If you can't access or underwrite those managers, public markets may be the better risk/reward tradeoff.

Now you understand the real distribution of private equity returns and why all private equity funds and deals are not golden. In the next chapter, we'll explore how PE deals actually get done and where they can go wrong.

PART II

SURVIVE AND THRIVE IN A PE PORTFOLIO COMPANY

"There is great chaos under heaven; the situation is excellent."

— MAO ZEDONG

CHAPTER 6

How Deals Get Done (And Where They Go Wrong)

I've seen advisors push deals too fast, ignoring signals that later became full-blown problems. Once you get into an actual deal, momentum takes over. People want to finish the deal, and they can compromise significantly on certain valuation and due-diligence concerns.

Speed and financial engineering can get in the way of deal success. The clock is always ticking, and due-diligence timelines can be very short—things can be overlooked, brushed aside, or moved through too quickly. Financial engineering and increased debt create risk. A deal may start with a level of debt that seems manageable. But if due diligence misses something, the market shifts, regulations change, or competitors prove tougher than expected, that leverage can quickly become unsustainable. And once it's locked in, it's hard to undo. This is what makes the nature of private equity quite risky—its emphasis on financial engineering and speed.

As a result, one out of ten portfolio companies bought by PE ends up in bankruptcy or financial restructuring. For some very aggressive firms, this number jumps to one in five.

In this chapter, we'll dissect the anatomy of a PE deal—examining how shortcuts, blind spots, and misaligned incentives can derail even the best-laid plans and lead to costly misfires.

The Speed Trap: When Urgency Overrides Due Diligence

The biggest pitfall in private equity is the speed trap. Urgency can override due diligence and create deal disasters. Private equity moves at the same relentless pace in closing deals as it does in running companies and driving to the exit. High-pressure timelines often rush the process, allowing red flags to slip through. If advisors skip the slow work, you inherit fast failure.

In due diligence, it's not enough to run through a checklist. Every deal has one, and every firm has its own master template. What matters is digging deeper—understanding the real issues, the risks beneath the surface, and the emotions driving decisions. That means building in structured pause points, taking the time to pressure-test assumptions, and running extensive scenario planning—both upside and downside—at every stage. Give dissidents a seat at the table. Have people play the devil's advocate and really test your assumptions. What if this went wrong? What if this didn't work?

I watched a deal pushed too quickly, only to see early, ignored warnings resurface as a crisis. I've seen this happen on regulatory issues, on IT issues, and on market assumptions—by pushing category growth rates and company share growth assumptions that were unrealistic. I've also seen situations where significant cost reductions were assumed to be easily achievable, but no one considered their impact on performance. The result was predictable—declining customer service and reduced capabilities that ultimately drove customers away.

Another specific deal stands out where due diligence moved too fast and critical issues were brushed aside. After closing, two areas became apparent very quickly. One was the regulatory environment changing and becoming more adverse, which increased taxes and lowered the overall EBITDA significantly. The other piece was marketplace trends that didn't just slow down but became significantly negative post-closing. This was something that could have been modeled out as part of scenario planning (especially given historical industry cycles) but was never looked at in detail. The deal was greatly affected by preventable oversights.

Communication Collapse: Why Silence Kills Deals Faster Than Sabotage

Another area where deals can unravel is in communication collapse. Deals fall apart faster from silence than sabotage. Undercommunication of risks and assumptions breeds mistrust, especially across internal and external teams, because of the pressures of the clock, the exit, and performance. There's a tendency for operating company leadership to constantly reinforce the progress being made on performance and toward the exit. When risks or challenges arise, they're often hard to voice; management fears falling behind the exit timeline and the consequences that come with it. Left unaddressed, those risks can escalate, eroding confidence in the leadership team.

That's why openly addressing risks as they come up is crucial. Running a PE-backed business requires never-ending due diligence—constantly reassessing the landscape. And as risks grow in magnitude, they must be communicated quickly and clearly to preserve confidence between the PE firm and the leadership team. Once credibility fractures, no spreadsheet can rebuild it. It is imperative to overcommunicate risks and reasoning early, often, and in plain language.

Most risks follow patterns you can see in a company's history—looking back helps you model what could go wrong. I've seen a deal leader under-communicate those risks to stakeholders, lose trust midway, and end up with a deal thesis that was neither makeable nor sustainable. Transparency is not a liability; it's a differentiator.

Financial Engineering Over Operational Reality

It's also important to ensure you don't fall into the trap of pushing financial engineering over everything. Financial engineering often trumps operational insight in deal-making. PE firms sometimes prioritize debt structure, tax efficiency, and exit math over long-term business viability. When that happens, they risk overlooking competitive and market dynamics that can trip them up later.

Some studies show that as much as half of PE firms' value creation can be due to leverage. When leverage jumps from 25% of the balance sheet to 50% or more, equity returns multiply, and value creation accelerates. But debt should never be the primary driver of value. Overly aggressive firms that rely too heavily on financial engineering often experience significantly more of their companies going into bankruptcy or financial restructuring—sometimes as high as one in five. The focus must stay on operational improvements and building a stronger business, not just on balance sheet manipulation.

When financial tactics ignore operating realities, the business pays later. Seasoned operational leaders must be integrated early to test structural assumptions. Spreadsheets can suggest sweeping cost cuts or restructures, but without industry expertise, those assumptions rarely hold. That's why the insight and capability of the operating team are critical.

It is critical to bring operating leaders into due diligence early. Their insight ensures that operating structures are realistic, growth is achievable, and the value case is built on substance—not weakened by blind cost-cutting.

BUSINESS CASE

EXCESSIVE FINANCIAL ENGINEERING

Few examples illustrate the perils of aggressive financial engineering better than Payless ShoeSource. Once a household name in affordable footwear, Payless became a casualty of leveraged buyout dynamics that prioritized extraction over reinvestment. The company's story shows how heavy debt loads and dividend recaps can erode a brand's ability to adapt—turning a defensible business into a cautionary tale within a decade.

In 2012, Payless was acquired for roughly $2 billion by Golden Gate Capital and Blum Capital Partners. The leveraged buyout saddled Payless with debt estimated to have risen from about $125 million pre-deal to over $400 million post-transaction.

Over the next several years, the PE owners reportedly extracted between $350 million and $400 million in dividends through debt-financed recapitalizations, shifting cash out of the business rather than into it.

This left Payless ill-equipped to confront the sweeping retail transformation of the 2010s. As digital commerce surged and competitors like Amazon, Walmart, and Target invested heavily in omnichannel strategies, Payless struggled to modernize its stores or build a viable e-commerce platform. Margins shrank while interest expenses mounted. By early 2017, burdened by about $838 million in debt, Payless filed for Chapter 11 bankruptcy, closing nearly 700 stores as part of its restructuring. Though the company emerged later that year with reduced debt and a slimmed-down footprint, its turnaround was short-lived.

By February 2019, Payless filed for bankruptcy again, this time liquidating its 2,100 remaining North American stores and laying off approximately 16,000 employees. Despite brand recognition and a solid value proposition, the business had been financially hollowed out. Its balance sheet—bloated with debt and drained by recaps—had become as constraining as its outdated store base. The lack of capital investment in online infrastructure, customer engagement, and inventory systems proved fatal in a retail environment that rewarded adaptability.

What makes the Payless case so instructive is that the company's fundamentals were never fatally flawed. Affordable footwear and broad appeal gave it a defendable niche. But instead of directing cash toward modernization or digital transformation, the owners prioritized short-term liquidity events.

The resulting cycle of underinvestment, declining store quality, and eroding customer loyalty left Payless unable to compete on experience or convenience.

The broader lesson is clear: financial engineering can amplify returns in the short run, but if pursued without operational renewal, it accelerates decline. Leveraged buyouts that emphasize extraction over reinvestment can destroy both equity value and livelihoods. In Payless's case, a classic American retailer—once serving millions of budget-conscious families—was liquidated entirely, leaving creditors and employees to absorb the cost of a strategy focused more on leverage than leadership.

The Math Only Works If The Machine Does

In the end, a PE firm must excel at fundraising and deliver strong net returns after fees. To do this, each firm develops its own playbook—how it uses leverage, drives value, and manages its checklists. That creates distinct operating cultures across firms. From the outside, the machine looks similar, but the methods each firm uses to raise capital and generate returns can differ in meaningful ways. Different PE firms have different operating cultures and processes. Invest in, work with, or sell to the firm that best matches your expectations and requirements.

KEY CHAPTER TAKEAWAYS

1. Momentum Can Blind You
- Once a deal is in motion, urgency pushes people to ignore red flags.
- Advisors and executives may rationalize away risks just to reach closing.

2. The Speed Trap Is Real
- High-pressure timelines rush diligence and let weak assumptions slide.
- Structured pause points, scenario planning, and devil's advocates protect against blind spots.

3. Communication Failures Kill Deals
- Silence on risks erodes trust faster than outright sabotage.
- Continuous, candid updates preserve credibility between PE firms and operators.

4. Over-Reliance on Financial Engineering Is Dangerous
- Leverage may create quick value but masks operational weaknesses.
- When markets shift, debt magnifies the downside far faster than the upside.

5. Bankruptcy Rates Are High for a Reason
- Roughly one in ten PE-owned companies end up in financial restructuring; aggressive firms see closer to one in five.
- Excessive leverage and shallow due diligence are the common culprits.

6. Operations Must Check the Math
- Financial models mean little without operational validation.
- Integrating operating leaders early ensures value cases aren't built on spreadsheets alone.

7. Payless as a Warning Sign
- Heavy dividend recaps and ignored digital shifts drove Payless from LBO to liquidation.
- Financial extractions starved the business just as consumer expectations were evolving.

8. Risks Follow Historical Patterns
- Most "surprise" risks could have been seen in past market, regulatory, or company trends.
- Mining history and pattern recognition strengthens diligence and future-proofing.

9. Each Firm Has Its Own Playbook
- While PE models share core mechanics, every firm applies its own flavor of checklists, leverage, and operating tactics.
- Understanding a specific firm's culture helps predict how they'll run and exit deals.

10. The Math Only Works If the Machine Does
- Fundraising, leverage, and deal structures only pay off if the portfolio machine delivers.
- Discipline in diligence and operating execution makes the math real instead of theoretical.

Knowing where deals fail is just the start. In the next chapter, we'll look at valuation and due diligence in more detail and why the price you pay is only the beginning of the real cost.

CHAPTER 7

From Price to Pitfall— Cracking PE Valuation and Due Diligence

I once believed in discounted cash flows and clean comps. Then I watched a PE firm stretch valuation logic to justify a high bid, knowing it would hurt later.

When a PE firm projects rising volumes, soaring margins, massive cost synergies, and promises it will all happen in six to twelve months—without management turnover or organizational friction—you can be sure the valuation is cooked. I've seen deals built on unrealistic growth rates and category assumptions, as if competitors would simply stand aside.

In this chapter, we'll break down how valuation really works in private equity—why it's more art than science, and how firms often use due diligence not to confirm the price but to justify it. By definition, your valuation will always be wrong, and your due diligence will always miss. The key to a successful deal is the degree of error on both.

Start Valuation And Due Diligence Assuming The Worst

For valuation, it's extremely important to start with a worst case as the base case and build from there. Start with history—study the company's tough periods and times when the market slowed and recognize those conditions can return. Then build your valuation on a series of executable building blocks, each with probabilities assigned. Nothing ever plays out exactly as planned, but this approach gives you the most realistic framework for a credible valuation range. The valuation illusion happens when valuations are reverse-engineered to match the desired bid. Once a deal gathers momentum, it's hard to stop. Valuations often shift toward best-case assumptions to push the deal through. When negatives emerge, they're papered over with optimistic forecasts rather than grounded in history or executable building blocks.

On due diligence, perform a ten-year-plus scan of the history of the company, the industry, and its competitors. Focus on regulatory, consumer, customer, marketplace shifts, and competitive reactions. Look at the good and the bad. Use that as an opportunity to ensure you really get under the skin of the due diligence and retest things that can and almost certainly will go wrong again.

The Model Follows The Motive

PE firms often lean on earnings before interest, taxes, depreciation, and amortization (EBITDA) multiples and stretch logic to win deals, even when discounted cash flow tells a different story.

In theory, discounted cash flow (DCF) is the correct valuation method. But in practice, firms default to comparable EBITDA multiples to simplify and justify pricing. Used conservatively, it can work—but more often, the search is for higher multiples to support the valuation already in mind and what is needed to complete a deal.

If you trust the model without questioning its motives, you're buying fiction. Instead, you should rebuild the logic backward and challenge assumptions, rather than anchor in what the exit math demands. Rebuild the valuation backward in a way that gives you a solid roadmap to the exit plan. Understand the actual building blocks that take you from where the business is today toward the exit plan. Include potential negatives and assign realistic probabilities to your likelihood of executing each building block, even with regulatory changes or competitive reaction.

I've seen private equity firms inflate comps and overlook DCF warnings to justify overreaching bids. It always comes back to assumptions—when every one of them is positive: market growth, share gains, big synergies, falling costs, and no organizational friction. That's the hallmark of an overvalued deal.

Unfortunately, the model often follows the motive, not the market. Don't let valuation and diligence become exercises in justifying a deal or confirming a story you want to believe. And do not view the company as you wish it were. Dig beneath the surface and test how it will perform in the real market, with real customers and real competitors.

Beyond The Comparable Multiple Trap

It is unwise to blindly follow a single EBITDA multiple. Find four or five solid comparable transactions from real deals—and then look deeper. What returns did those deals generate? How does their risk profile compare to the company in front of you? And how has the market environment shifted since? Regulatory pressures and competitive intensity today may be very different from when those comps were done even a few years ago.

Build conservatism and skepticism into every valuation—because not everything will go right. Even with cautious assumptions, surprises will emerge that drag value down. Don't blindly follow the model; understand the drivers beneath it. Rebuild the logic backward, challenge assumptions, and anchor in what the exit math demands.

One approach is to forget the multiple and start from scratch—assume everything goes wrong. Use history as your guide to build that worst-case scenario. From there, layer in specific value-creation strategies, block by block, assigning probabilities to each. Add potential setbacks—competitive threats, regulatory surprises, market declines—and model those as well. This method produces a far stronger, more realistic valuation than relying on multiples alone.

Diligence Or Decoration

Too often, due diligence turns into performance art—checking boxes without changing minds. Every firm has its checklist, but real diligence goes far beyond ticking items off a list. It's about uncovering what truly matters: understanding the company's past decade, its competitors, and its industry, then pressure-testing the future through scenario planning and trend analysis. That deeper investigation delivers far more insight than any box-checking exercise ever could.

The real due diligence is uncovering weak links, inflated forecasts, hidden integration cost risk, market risk, overly aggressive pricing assumptions, and potential regulatory issues. Again, you can look at some of that historically—a lot of it has probably already happened at some point in a different way. You can also look at the future and what could go wrong. Surface-level reviews create blind spots that explode post-close. You have to get beneath the surface of due diligence and truly understand each area—only then can you see the full range of what might go wrong.

Another factor people often underestimate is competitive reaction. In capitalism, success invites imitation—if you do something that wins with consumers or customers, competitors will either copy it or counter it with something new. That reality must be built into due diligence, because no strategy lives in a vacuum.

It is helpful to build adversarial reviews. Have one team challenge every core assumption with skin in the game. Don't be afraid to challenge every single assumption. Have someone play the devil's advocate and figure out what's really going wrong. Have your best, brightest, and most cynical team members sit across the table from you and challenge each of your assumptions, both the positive and the negative, and brainstorm what else could happen. Make sure they're fully briefed on the historical context, as well as the future risks and warning signs management has already identified. Taking this contrarian view seriously can spark excellent discussions that challenge and refine the assumptions underlying due diligence.

EBITDA Games And Financial Sleight of Hand

I've seen a CFO that trusted the comps and got crushed when diligence missed historical EBITDA games.

EBITDA is often "adjusted" with the claim that certain positives will last, certain negatives won't repeat, or future improvements are guaranteed. In practice, these adjustments recur year after year—just in different forms. Exercise caution with both adjusted and reported EBITDA. Look beneath the numbers for hidden issues—product loading, inventory run-downs, or short-term swings in payables and receivables. These can distort results, but they can be uncovered and addressed through thorough due diligence.

Reported EBITDA, or even adjusted EBITDA, can differ sharply from actual performance. The key is to break down the elements: what's included in adjusted EBITDA and how EBITDA lines up with cash flow. Even cash flow can be manipulated through shifts in inventory, receivables, or payables. That's why it's essential to study long-term trends, understand what's driving the changes, and separate true one-offs from recurring adjustments. Many so-called one-offs actually occur every year—they're simply part of doing business, even if materially negative.

The Prettiest Pitch Decks Hide The Messiest Truths

I've seen two-hundred-page business plan decks filled with pains-taking detail—by product, by region, by plant. Yet beneath the surface, they were built on overly optimistic and poorly tested assumptions. Some decks looked perfect on paper: record category growth, expanding market share, rising margins, flawless synergies, and seamless cost cuts. In reality, few of those projections held up. Competitors pushed back, customers resisted, consumers proved fickle, and employees hesitated. Those real-world reactions must always be factored into any plan.

The quality of the valuation, the investment thesis, and the due diligence has nothing to do with the amount of paper or the length of the deck. When you see decks that stack three or four positive assumptions together, the benefits and valuation become exponential, especially when detailed at the product level, by geographic segment. The overwhelming detail doesn't validate the assumptions. Separate the length of the deck and quality of the presentation from the quality of the thinking and understanding of the underlying valuation.

The cost of ignorance here is steep. The biggest deals unravel due to due-diligence gaps around margin pressure and market fit. What aren't always seen are market shifts in the consumer landscape, assuming what happened in the past will exponentially continue without any competitive reaction. When these market shifts happen in private equity, there's usually a need for increased investment, more innovation, and longer exit timelines to match those shifts. When those are missed, there can be huge differences in value created and exit timing.

DUE DILIGENCE FAILURE MIXED WITH AGGRESSIVE PE TACTICS

Prospect Medical Holdings offers a stark example of how aggressive financial extraction layered onto weak fundamentals—and inadequate due diligence—can push a mission-critical business into collapse. This is less a story of operational failure than one of structural fragility exposed by strategic overreach.

In 2010, Leonard Green & Partners acquired a controlling stake in Prospect for approximately $363 million, gaining ownership of a hospital chain serving safety-net and low-income communities across multiple states. Over the following decade, the firm extracted an estimated $658 million in dividends and fees while restructuring the company's assets in ways that undermined long-term viability.

One of the most consequential moves was the sale-leaseback of nearly all hospital real estate to Medical Properties Trust for more than $1.4 billion. The transaction locked the hospitals into triple-net leases, requiring them to pay rent, insurance, and maintenance on properties they once owned outright. This transformed previously owned assets into fixed financial obligations—an unsustainable burden for facilities already operating on razor-thin margins.

In 2018, Prospect borrowed roughly $457 million to fund another large dividend payment, even as the company reported significant operating losses. With rising interest costs, deferred maintenance, and aging equipment, hospitals struggled to maintain patient care standards. Service lines were cut, physician turnover accelerated, and community trust eroded.

By January 2025, Prospect filed for Chapter 11 bankruptcy, weighed down by billions in debt and an eroding operating base. The collapse left a trail of unpaid taxes, lawsuits, and shuttered hospitals, drawing intense political and public backlash. State lawmakers introduced—but failed to pass—reforms aimed at curbing similar private equity practices in healthcare, leaving affected communities with fewer hospitals and heavier taxpayer burdens.

The most visible failure, however, lay in due diligence. A deeper assessment of Prospect's operations at acquisition would have revealed systemic issues: high dependence on government reimbursements, outdated billing systems, chronic staff turnover, and limited capital investment capacity. These were structural risks that leverage and lease obligations only magnified. Once the balance sheet was strained, the underlying business had no cushion left.

The broader lesson is clear: due diligence must go far beyond financial modeling. It's not enough to validate revenue and margin forecasts; investors must interrogate the real drivers of stability—regulatory exposure, workforce health, technology, and customer trust. In highly leveraged environments, every unasked question can become a future crisis. The Prospect collapse reminds investors that the cheapest form of insurance in any deal is rigorous diligence up front—because once leverage is applied, even small blind spots can destroy an entire investment.

PAYING PEAK PRICES FOR DIGITAL DECLINE

Terra Firma's acquisition of EMI Group remains one of the most infamous examples of private equity overreach—a case where paying a peak-cycle price for a structurally declining industry destroyed billions in investor capital.

In 2007, Terra Firma Capital Partners, led by Guy Hands, acquired EMI Group for approximately £4.2 billion ($6.5 billion), narrowly outbidding rivals in a fiercely contested auction. The deal was financed with more than £3 billion in debt provided largely by Citigroup, leaving a thin equity cushion of roughly £1.75 billion. Terra Firma's thesis hinged on the assumption that the decline in compact disc sales had bottomed out, and that better management, cost control, and digital strategy could restore EMI's profitability.

But the timing couldn't have been worse. The global music industry was in structural freefall, as digital downloads, piracy, and the emergence of streaming decimated physical sales faster than expected. EMI's legacy infrastructure and heavy debt load left little room for adaptation. Cash flow deteriorated, and high interest payments absorbed capital that could have funded innovation. The loss of marquee acts such as Radiohead and The Rolling Stones, both of whom left amid creative and financial disputes, further damaged morale and brand equity.

When the 2008–09 financial crisis struck, Terra Firma's over-leveraged structure became untenable. EMI breached its loan covenants in 2010, and after failed attempts to renegotiate terms, Citigroup seized control in February 2011, writing off about £2.2 billion in debt and wiping out Terra Firma's entire equity stake. The storied label was subsequently broken up and sold—with Universal Music Group acquiring its recorded music division and Sony/ATV (with Michael Jackson's estate) taking the publishing arm.

The EMI collapse underscores how financial modeling can obscure strategic reality. Terra Firma's forecasts assumed stabilization in a market still in freefall, overestimated management's ability to pivot digitally, and underestimated the cultural complexity of managing artists in transition. As one of the first major private equity bets on a creative industry, it also revealed how standard LBO mechanics—high leverage, aggressive projections, and financial engineering—can backfire in sectors driven by talent and technology disruption rather than scale and efficiency.

The broader lesson is timeless: even iconic brands can't defy structural decline or justify peak-cycle pricing. A model may show clean IRRs, strong coverage ratios, and optimistic margin lifts—but if those numbers aren't supported by a detailed, high-probability operational plan, they're fiction. Deals that depend on flawless execution in volatile industries are time bombs. The spreadsheet may balance, but the market doesn't lie.

UNDERSTANDING VALUATION IN PRIVATE EQUITY: EBITDA MULTIPLES VS. DISCOUNTED CASH FLOW (DCF)

Valuation is at the heart of every private equity deal. The price a firm pays on entry largely determines potential returns at exit. In practice, private equity relies on two principal tools: comparable company EBITDA multiples and the discounted cash flow (DCF) method. Multiples dominate because they are simple, fast, and grounded in market evidence, but DCF serves as a critical check to ensure the numbers hold up under scrutiny.

What EBITDA Is and Why It Matters—EBITDA stands for Earnings Before Interest, Taxes, Depreciation, and Amortization. It is not a GAAP (generally accepted accounting principle) measure, but rather a financial shorthand designed to highlight the company's operating performance without the distortions of:

- Financing choices (interest expense depends on debt levels)
- Tax regimes (companies across geographies face different effective tax rates)
- Accounting policies (depreciation and amortization vary depending on asset base and assumptions)

For PE investors, EBITDA is useful because it approximates a company's cash-generating capacity from operations, which is the fuel that services debt, funds growth, and drives equity returns. There is one catch: it also eliminates depreciation. This can be misleading for companies that require heavy, new operating investments or capital expenditures—either because of their business model or because they are catching up on delayed investments. This can be addressed by also completing a robust DCF forecast.

Unlike net income, which can swing dramatically due to capital structure, EBITDA allows investors to compare companies on a like-for-like basis. This is particularly important in private equity, where most transactions involve adding leverage, and where isolating the underlying business performance is key.

Comparable EBITDA Multiples: The Industry Standard— The most common approach for PE is to value companies based on comparable EBITDA multiples. The logic is straightforward: similar businesses should trade at similar multiples of their operating profits (EBITDA is technically operating profits before depreciation and amortization).

PE firms build a comparative set of companies (comp sets) using two lenses:

1. **Public comps:** listed peers in the same sector (e.g., Chipotle or Shake Shack for fast-casual dining).
2. **Precedent transactions:** prices paid in recent M&A deals involving similar businesses.

These comparables are adjusted for differences in scale, growth trajectory, margin profile, customer base, and geography. For example, a smaller regional player may trade at a discount to a national chain because of lower brand recognition and scalability. For most valuations, a comparable set of five or more companies is used.

Example: Suppose a target restaurant chain generates $50 million of EBITDA. After reviewing public comps and recent deals, the PE team sees a range of 8x to 12x forward EBITDA, with the median at 10x.

Resulting calculation: Enterprise Value (EV) = $50m × 10x = $500 million

Further adjustments might be made if the target is growing faster than peers (justifying a premium multiple) or is more operationally challenged (requiring a discount).

The Role of Discounted Cash Flow (DCF)—While comparative multiples dominate discussions, sophisticated investors run a DCF as a cross-check. Unlike multiples, which assume the market is pricing peers correctly, the DCF looks inward at the company's own ability to generate cash over time (including needed capital expenditures).

How a DCF Works:

1. **Project Free Cash Flow (FCF):** Start with EBITDA, subtract expected capital expenditures, changes in working capital, and taxes to estimate future FCF.
2. **Apply a Discount Rate:** Use the weighted average cost of capital (WACC) to reflect both the risk of the business and the cost of financing.

3. **Calculate Terminal Value:** Since most value comes from the years beyond the explicit forecast, a terminal value is estimated, usually using an exit multiple of EBITDA.
4. **Add It Up:** The sum of discounted cash flows plus terminal value gives total enterprise value.

Continuing the restaurant chain example:

- Forecast average annual FCF: $40m over the next 5 years.
- Discounted back at 10%, this equals ~$150m.
- Add a terminal value (using a 10x multiple on year-five EBITDA of $60m = $600m, discounted back to ~$350m).
- Total EV ≈ $500m, which matches the market-based multiple approach.

Here, the DCF confirms that the EBITDA multiple valuation is reasonable. If the DCF had suggested only $400m, the PE team might question whether paying 10x was justified.

- DCF suggests enterprise value of $500m.
- If financed with $300m debt and $200m equity, entry equity value = $200m.
- At exit, if EV grows to $700m and debt is reduced to $250m, equity value = $450m.
- That's a 2.25x multiple on invested equity, showing how leverage amplifies returns.

Example With Debt Layer:

- Debt magnifies returns: less equity upfront means higher equity multiples if EV grows.

- DCF checks assume leverage must be serviceable: even if enterprise value looks good, cash flows must cover debt.
- Exit valuations are equity-focused: enterprise value minus debt at exit is what investors actually realize.

Why This Matters in PE: In private equity, DCFs can be structured in two main ways:

Unlevered DCF (Enterprise Value Approach):

- Start with EBITDA, subtract taxes, capital expenditures, and working capital → unlevered free cash flow (UFCF).
- Discount these cash flows at the weighted average cost of capital (WACC), which blends cost of debt and equity.
- This gives enterprise value (EV). Subtract net debt (debt minus cash) to reach equity value.
- Levered DCF (Equity Value Approach):
- Start with cash flows after interest and debt repayments.
- Discount at the cost of equity.
- This produces equity value directly.

Unlevered DCF is the most common in PE because it values the business independent of financing structure, while levered DCF is useful for modeling specific equity returns.

Summary

- EBITDA multiples serve as the common language of the private equity industry. They anchor valuations in real market activity and provide a clear, practical basis for negotiation.

- Although multiples are easier to calculate and provide real-world grounding, they can overlook actual or future cash-flow pressures—especially those caused by required new investments (such as capital expenditures) or by financing structures.
- DCF provides a deeper, intrinsic perspective, ensuring valuations are supported by actual cash-flow generation, not just market comparables.
- PE investors balance the two: multiples set the benchmark, DCF checks the logic, and judgment bridges the gap.

Ultimately, valuation is as much art as science. The right number reflects both what the business is worth and what the market is willing to pay. For PE firms, mastering both EBITDA multiples and DCF, along with thoughtful due diligence, is essential to disciplined investing

KEY CHAPTER TAKEAWAYS

1. The Model Follows the Motive

- When bids stretch, assumptions "magically" improve—margins rise, volumes jump, synergies arrive on cue.
- Treat any forecast stacking multiple positives with no friction as a valuation red flag.

2. Start from "Worst Case as Base Case"

- Anchor on history's bad years, not the rosiest run-rate; then layer only high-probability value-creation blocks.
- Assign explicit probabilities to each driver; uncertainty priced in now is pain avoided later.

3. Multiples Are a Shortcut, Not a Truth

- Comparable EBITDA multiples can be cherry-picked or stale versus today's risk regime.
- Build a comp set (4–5+ real precedents), adjust for growth, margin, and risk. Then sanity-check against DCF.

4. DCF Is the Conscience of the Deal

- Use unlevered DCF to test intrinsic cash generation (including CapEx and working capital), not to "bless" a number.
- If DCF and market multiples diverge, interrogate assumptions—not the discount rate.

5. Reverse-Engineer to Exit Reality

- Work backward from the exit: likely buyer, realistic exit multiple, debt paydown path, and timing.
- If you can't map credible steps from today to sale, the price is fiction.

6. Diligence or Decoration?

- Checklists don't catch pattern risk—ten-year scans of industry, regulation, and competitor reactions do.
- Run adversarial reviews: assign a team to attack every core assumption with skin in the game.

7. Beware EBITDA Games

- "Adjusted" EBITDA often normalizes recurring negatives and one-offs that show up every year with new names.
- Tie EBITDA to cash: test for channel stuffing, inventory pulls, payables and receivables timing, and seasonality.

8. Competition Always Hits Back

- Forecasts that assume share gains without retaliation are storytelling, not underwriting.
- Bake in competitive countermoves (price, promotions, new innovations, expanded distribution, etc.) and re-rate the multiple accordingly.

9. Pretty Decks, Ugly Truths

- A two-hundred-page product-level plan can still sit on unrealistic category growth, margin lift, and "instant" synergies.
- Separate presentation polish from decision logic; reward evidence, not elegance.

10. Pay Up Only When the Machine Works

- Overpayment + leverage + structural headwinds = equity wipeouts, however clever the spreadsheet.
- Price discipline, probabilistic modeling, and hard-nosed diligence are the only antidotes to deal momentum.

Valuation gets the deal signed, but people you can bet on make it work. In the next chapter, we'll explore how to assemble a team that survives PE pressure before the firm assembles one for you.

CHAPTER **8**

Assembling a Winning Team (Before the PE Firm Assembles You)

I've sat in a boardroom where the founder no longer recognized half their executive team. They'd all been replaced post-close.

The founder didn't think the team going forward after private equity bought his company was important. For him, the most important thing was the paycheck. He later realized that the most critical decision was choosing a team capable of driving the performance culture needed for a PE-portfolio company.

It's never a good situation when the PE firm starts making personnel decisions for you. Suddenly, you have people inserted into the team who don't understand the culture you've built—placed there whether you agree or not. At the same time, they create new communication channels back to the PE firm, since they are seen as "their pick." The result is chaos: misalignment, disruption, and a breakdown in clear, consistent communication.

It's imperative that the leadership team—especially the operating company's leader—sets the agenda for the people on the team. That means making sure every member understands the culture expected by the PE firm, excels in their role, collaborates effectively, and keeps sight of the bigger picture.

In a PE-operating company environment, everything accelerates exponentially due to the unique nature of enhanced performance and speed mixed with the compressed exit timeline. Team mistakes—whether it's the wrong hire, poor performance, or lack of alignment—are magnified. The culture of speed demands alignment and momentum. Once someone falls behind, it disrupts performance and stretches the exit timeline, making recovery far more difficult.

In this chapter, you'll learn how to preemptively build the team you want before PE does it for you. It's not just about skill sets— it's about trust, resilience, and narrative control. It's also about making sure that the team can work together collaboratively and understands what's required of a PE culture versus a publicly owned company.

Build Your Team Before The Deal Closes

The most important thing you can do is to preemptively build your team before the deal closes. If you don't shape your leadership bench, the PE firm you're working with will do it for you. Firms often bring in operators or CFOs they trust, sometimes before they even close. It's critical to influence and shape the team you need to drive results, EBITDA, and cash flow. If you don't, you risk losing influence—or even being sidelined in your own company. Always remember: the PE firm holds majority ownership and they can make changes at any time.

If performance slips or the timeline drifts, the PE firm may decide they can move faster with someone else. That's when you risk being sidelined—decisions bypass you, shift to others, or you're replaced entirely. The only protection is transparent communication and staying on track with performance and timing. At the end of the day, the PE firm holds the authority to make unilateral changes.

Start your own leadership audit before the letter of intent is signed. Fill the gaps with people aligned to both you and the deal—people who can work in the extremely high-pressured, fast-paced culture needed in PE. Everything takes on a faster timeline. Begin assembling your team early. Bring people on board who can adapt quickly and immerse them in the culture so they understand what private equity demands. From that point forward, everyone must operate with urgency—driving the value-creation levers and pushing decisively toward the exit timeline.

You don't have time for office politics. You don't have time for people who cannot do their core jobs. You certainly don't have time for people straying away from the main strategies and value levers of the company. It's important to keep the group moving fast and in the same direction as quickly as possible.

In one deal I was involved with, an operator negotiated two to three specific team members into the agreement from the beginning—people he knew could drive excellent results based on previous collaborations. By involving them upfront, he saved enormous time and addressed key value levers in supply chain, marketing, finance, and cost structure from day one. This exemplifies a founder or CEO driving the process of assembling the right team, rather than letting the process drive him.

Clarify And Manage Operating Partners

The PE firm will most likely assign an operating partner to work with the leadership team (a professional in the private equity firm who focuses on the operational management and improvement of portfolio companies—think of them as a consultant who actually owns your business). Not all operating partners are team players when it comes to culture in a portfolio company. Some add genuine value, while others sow confusion, duplicate roles, or drive wedges between the leaders and the team. Remember, a team member who doesn't understand the culture and fails to add value hurts a PE-portfolio company exponentially harder due to the compressed timeline and the crunch schedules required to reach exit. There's no room for having the wrong players on the team; you don't have the time for that luxury given the exit pressure.

You must have clarity on who the operating partner is, what their mandate includes, and how they'll integrate with your existing structure. I've seen a CEO successfully negotiate operating partner involvement directly into the term sheet, which avoided potential future confusion and power struggles.

The CFO As Your Strategic Shield

I've advised a founder before to hire a PE-savvy CFO, and it protected them. Post-close, one of the most important positions in a PE-portfolio company after the CEO is the CFO. This pressure comes from the intense metric and reporting requirements, and the relentless focus on EBITDA and cash flow—both of which must be driven and tracked by the CEO and CFO together. The CFO is one of the most critical roles on a portfolio company's leadership team. While they may not do all the work themselves, they are responsible for keeping everything on track and ensuring key metrics are reported with precision.

The right CFO will partner with both the portfolio-company CEO and the PE firm, making the entire process as seamless as possible. That CFO should understand the unique PE requirements, hit the ground running, and implement the necessary reporting requirements and cash flow focus from day one. The CFO also has to be on the watch for financial surprises—inventory bloat or unexpected cost increases. This allows the CEO to concentrate on the value levers in the company rather than getting bogged down in every operational detail.

The Three Non-Negotiable Cultural Requirements

When I think about people culture in a PE environment, I require three non-negotiables from each team member. First, they need to excel at their core job with speed under pressure. That's absolutely critical. Only they are uniquely qualified to do that. Second, they must understand the total PE culture and business from a commercial standpoint, including how to drive cash flow and EBITDA within the broader business. Third, they need to be collaborative—working toward the same team objective, same culture, and same exit timeline with everyone else. These are the three essential requirements.

If your existing team doesn't trust the new faces and doubts that a team member can deliver on those three elements, execution will stall. Some team members may create confusion and generate noise instead of results. Some fall into analysis paralysis, which, in a PE environment, is deadly.

If you're going to analyze something, do it quickly. Establish decision trees and collaborative frameworks where small and medium decisions are made rapidly. Large decisions should be discussed and resolved within weeks, not months. Minor decisions should be made in hours or days. If you have a team member who wants to analyze everything without making decisions or taking calculated risks, that person can severely slow the process and create significant obstacles.

The wrong help at the wrong time creates drag, not lift. When you get the wrong help (someone working against value-creation levers, the timeline to exit, or generating noise instead of forward momentum), there's an exponential negative impact. There's no right time for the wrong help, but in PE timelines with added exit pressure, any wrong help can be catastrophic.

Protecting Culture Under Compressed Timelines

You must watch cultural carve-outs carefully. Team changes don't just shift workflows—they reshuffle culture entirely. When you change a team member, the integration process of understanding workflows, adapting to culture, learning the business, and building relationships must happen at an accelerated pace due to timing constraints. New leaders bring fresh energy but also risk misaligning values, damaging morale, or delaying critical initiatives needed for exit success.

When a private equity–operated company is working properly, its culture becomes a finely tuned machine. People understand the clock. They understand the exit and the value levers. They execute with speed and precision. They make decisions and move forward.

If you introduce someone to that leadership team who doesn't fit that culture, the disruption can be devastating to your timeline and therefore to your ultimate success.

In a private equity environment, changes in people can change culture much faster because you're operating on a compressed timeline. This makes it critical to ensure every person fits in, can do their job well, collaborates effectively, and understands both the big picture and the PE culture. Cultural fractures become performance fractures, given the timing, intensity, and pressure everyone operates under.

For a well-run team, define your cultural non-negotiables and ensure any new leader is briefed on them. They should understand the private equity model and how different it is—how much more intense and short-term it is than the public ownership model. I've been in a situation where a CEO created a culture memo and made it part of the onboarding for new executives and PE partners. It's about being crystal clear on what's expected from a cultural standpoint in the PE environment, and making sure people understand it when they join the company.

Culture isn't a vibe; it's a brief. It's something that is absolutely required to realize the value in the short time needed to reach exit. It's not something that's nice to have. It's not something you kind of measure and hope gets better. Everybody's got to be on the same page. Everybody's got to be driving forward collaboratively to create value.

Compensation As Your Leadership Armor

The other important concept is using compensation for the portfolio leadership team as armor. A great team without the right incentives is a short-term asset and will not get you to exit or create the value that's needed. Management equity plans (known as MEPs) and annual compensation packages are often skewed in the PE firm's favor unless negotiated with outside professional help by the leaders of the portfolio company.

If your leadership team is unclear about the upside for them or if their annual cash compensation is weak, they'll be distracted, disengaged, and poached. In reality, the annual compensation package and the management equity plan represent a very small part of the total value being created in the whole deal, yet it can make the difference between a deal's success and failure. Therefore, the PE firm should take these plans seriously.

Before signing a letter of intent, hire an experienced compensation advisor to structure a management equity plan that rewards performance, vests sensibly, and aligns with exit goals while maximizing base salaries, bonuses, and benefits.

I worked with a CEO who secured a richer MEP and stronger cash compensation for their executives. This locked in loyalty through a turbulent hold period. The key here is that the difference in what was negotiated—the richer MEP and the improved cash compensation for the company leaders—was a small percentage of the total value created by the deal. Well-paid leaders fight harder and stay longer when the storm hits, and the storm always hits.

In private equity's high-performance environment, people must do their jobs well, be collaborative, understand the big picture, and drive toward a fairly quick timeline. These high-caliber people have many opportunities outside the company. If they're working in a public company, they receive annual equity grants for stock options or restricted shares, and they typically earn higher salaries and bonuses than in a private equity environment. The competition is fierce.

People can be poached or choose to leave for a public company, or another PE-owned firm, especially since exits often take five to seven years and the equity payout is uncertain. It's critical to stay closely attuned: if your team members are the right people and performing well, they must be compensated accordingly. They're giving up short-term equity for very long-term equity in one hit that may or may not be successful. This makes the risk higher on the equity side than in a public-company environment. Therefore, ensure that there's a high probability of getting that equity, and you must ensure that short-term cash compensation is excellent.

DEEP DIVE

LEADERSHIP, CULTURE, AND GOVERNANCE IN PE

When a company is bought by private equity, the spotlight almost always shifts to the numbers—leverage, EBITDA, margin expansion. But the truth is, the single biggest driver of success or failure is the **management team and the culture they create**. Price and diligence matter, but without the right leadership in place, the value-creation story falls apart quickly.

The challenge is that the PE model often collides with existing company culture. In particular, founder-led businesses struggle when a firm imposes quarterly board reporting, aggressive monthly KPI tracking, and a "do more with less" mindset. Longtime employees who thrived in an entrepreneurial environment suddenly feel like they're working for a micro-managing investment bank. That cultural whiplash leads to attrition, disengagement, and in some cases, outright resistance to change.

PE firms try to solve this by quickly installing executives they trust—sometimes former operators from their network, sometimes managers from other portfolio companies. This can often backfire. Dropping in a CEO or CFO who doesn't understand the industry or who clashes with the existing team creates chaos. Even management equity plans, which are designed to align incentives, can cause resentment if they're overly complex or create unequal rewards across the leadership team.

The best outcomes happen when PE firms strike a balance: respecting the strengths of the existing culture while introducing professionalization where it's truly needed. That often means keeping key executives and managers in place, giving them meaningful equity, and supporting them with the right operating partners and outside resources. At the end of the day, **the numbers only move if the people move**—and too many deals underestimate how hard it is to get culture and leadership right under the pressure cooker of PE ownership.

The first shock most CEOs feel after a private equity takeover is how fast and forcefully decisions get made. Public companies have layers of committees, shareholder votes, and regulatory checks that slow everything down. In private equity, none of that exists. The board is small, the owners are in the room, and they can replace leadership or pivot strategy overnight. For some executives, that's liberating. For others, it's brutal.

PE firms typically bring in **professional management processes:** weekly cash-flow forecasts, detailed KPI dashboards, board reporting packs, and regular reviews with the deal team. At best, these create focus and discipline. At worst, they create a spreadsheet-driven culture where every decision is about short-term EBITDA. Leaders who are used to autonomy suddenly find themselves questioned on every line item, and initiatives that don't show near-term ROI (return on investment) are quickly cut.

The governance model is also very different. The PE firm has the right to fire management at any time, and they use that power often. This keeps executives on edge and ensures performance pressure stays high. It also means the CEO's job is less about setting long-term vision and more about hitting targets in the next twelve to twenty-four months. For employees lower down, this can feel like whiplash: one quarter the focus is growth, the next it's cost-cutting. By year three, the entire leadership team may have turned over.

There are upsides. PE-backed companies often adopt modern IT systems, upgrade processes, and professionalize HR, finance, and supply chain faster than public companies. The machine works when management teams adapt quickly, embrace data-driven decision-making, and align tightly with the PE firm's expectations. But for leaders who resist, the machine can feel cold, transactional, and relentless.

In short, entering a PE-portfolio company means entering a different operating reality. The pace is faster, the oversight is tighter, and the tolerance for mistakes is lower. Some thrive in that environment. Many don't.

KEY CHAPTER TAKEAWAYS

1. Build Your Team Before Close
- If you don't shape the bench pre-signing, the PE firm will—often fast and without your input.
- Start a leadership audit before the LOI (letter of intent) and line up candidates aligned to the deal and the clock.

2. Own the CFO Decision
- A PE-savvy CFO is your operating shield: cash, EBITDA, reporting, and board confidence.
- Hire (or upgrade) at deal close so day-one reporting and cash discipline don't derail value creation.

3. Control the Narrative Channels
- PE-inserted hires create extra "lines to the owner" that can fragment decision-making.
- Establish clear lines of communication: who speaks to whom, about what, and how often.

4. Three Cultural Non-Negotiables
- Perform your core role with speed under pressure; understand broader PE economics and commercial issues (cash flow, EBITDA); collaborate relentlessly.
- Brief every leader on these expectations up front. Remember: culture is a brief, not a vibe.

5. Hire for Pace, Not Just Pedigree
- PE compresses time—weak links compound quickly and stall exits.
- Make decisive calls on misfits in weeks, not quarters; analysis paralysis leads to value leakage.

6. Define the Operating Partner's Mandate
- Great operating partners unblock; bad ones add noise, duplicate roles, and slow decisions.
- Negotiate scope and integration in the term sheet to avoid power struggles later.

7. Compensation Is Leadership Armor
- Strong MEP plus top-tier cash keeps top players focused through turbulence and poaching.
- Use an independent compensation advisor to structure vesting, performance triggers, and tax outcomes.

8. Pay for What You Need to Win Now
- In PE, leaders trade steady, public-company equity for a single, uncertain payout.
- Offset risk with highly competitive salary and bonus and a credible path to realizing MEP value.

9. Protect Culture Under a Compressed Clock
- Every new leader reshuffles norms—onboard with a culture memo and clear performance expectations.
- Tie metrics to the clock so execution speeds up, not down.

10. Anticipate the Governance Reality
- Owners are in the room; pivots and replacements can be overnight.
- Stay ahead with transparent performance updates and a bench for critical roles.

With the right team and incentives in place, you're no longer reacting to pressure; you're directing it. Next, we'll explore how founder and leadership identity and emotion intersect with performance and how to keep your compass steady through the storm.

CHAPTER 9

Welcome to the Machine— Thriving After a PE Takeover

The culture shifted overnight when the private equity firm took control. By Monday morning's meeting, priorities were rewired, and it felt like working for an entirely different company. Everything changed the day the deal closed.

In this chapter, you'll get an unfiltered look at what changes post-acquisition—from culture to cadence—and how to adapt, lead, and stay sane under private equity ownership.

The Root Cause Forcing Immediate Culture Reset

To understand the private equity cultural reboot, you have to consider the basic root causes and outcomes of PE: the importance of EBITDA and cash flow, exit timing, and the clock. Those things come together to reboot the entire culture of acquired companies on day one.

It comes down to this: performance means moving EBITDA and cash flow consistently and with speed. It also means tracking and reporting progress on those metrics while moving toward the exit on time or even ahead of schedule. Underperformance on any of these elements means significantly more pressure: more reporting and more initiatives to generate cash—including incremental cost reductions in overhead and supply costs, incremental asset sales, and incremental management changes.

One meeting from the new PE firm can signal a total operating overhaul. PE firms often introduce dashboards, KPIs, and top-down reviews that reset decision-making overnight. If you don't plan ahead and adapt quickly, your influence and standing erode, regardless of past performance. The PE firm controls the company and has the majority of board seats. Their culture of performance, speed to exit, and aggressive reporting is non-negotiable.

They can sense if anyone on the management team—whether it's the CEO, CFO, or other key members—isn't aligned to that overall paradigm. If you're not bought into the culture or not pushing the agenda hard, you'll quickly get sidelined and potentially replaced. Learn the new metrics and scorecard fast and lead with numbers that matter to the new owners. Take time to plan out and build your new reporting system, your new metrics, and how you'll track the things that are important to the firm, namely EBITDA and cash flow.

I experienced the Monday meeting shock firsthand: a PE-imposed dashboard that shifted the entire company's priorities overnight.

The Immediate Transformation: When PE Takes Control

From the moment a private equity firm closes a deal, the company's world transforms overnight. There's no grace period, no gradual adjustment. The performance machine kicks in immediately.

Your first day at a PE-owned company is very different from your first day at a publicly traded company. In a public company, you spend your first day (and first weeks and months) trying to understand the culture and learn about the business, talking to people to grasp the strategy and direction. At a PE-portfolio company, there's no luxury of gradual understanding—the performance culture hits you immediately, and adaptation isn't optional.

Day one brings an avalanche of financial scrutiny: EBITDA analysis, cash-flow projections, cost-reduction initiatives, asset-optimization spreadsheets. This isn't a secondary priority while you learn the business; this becomes the business. Everything else is extracurricular activity. New language and fluency around these metrics become non-negotiable, and the shift in oversight is complete and instantaneous.

Here's what separates the leaders who thrive from those who get crushed: getting out ahead of it. The PE firm is coming whether you're ready or not. They want EBITDA and cash-flow metrics, cost-reduction progress, and tight management of inventories, accounts payable, and receivables. You can either scramble to catch up to their demands or set up your own efficient but thorough oversight and reporting mechanisms before they ask.

Life becomes exponentially easier when you plan ahead and understand what the PE firm wants and needs, and set up your financial systems and reporting infrastructure to deliver that data. When you do this, both parties will be looking at the same sets of data. You're not chasing the numbers; you're providing them on a timely basis. You can course correct when pieces of the data don't show the progress you want, rather than spending all your time trying to create the data from scratch.

The End Of Management Autonomy

The autonomy your management team once enjoyed disappears almost instantly. Heads of sales and operations often struggle with dashboard-driven oversight and real-time scrutiny. What used to be workflow issues like lagging visibility or reporting delays now become performance red flags. PE firms get nervous if they don't have numbers steadily and readily available on a timely basis.

With this in mind, build reporting fluency and clean data infrastructure before scrutiny intensifies. Plan ahead on what drives cash flow and EBITDA. Get metrics and reporting in place and make sure it's timely and regular (weekly and monthly) before the pressure mounts.

I've seen a head of sales who couldn't adjust to the new oversight cadence and was replaced. He cratered under the immense pressure of monthly and quarterly targets, with sales being tracked daily, weekly, and monthly. Short-term reporting and the need for immediate fixes eroded his autonomy and kept him from focusing on what he did best, which was driving sales and building a team. Over time, the growing burden of metrics and reporting pulled him away from what truly mattered—being in the market, engaging with customers, spending time in stores, and driving the business for long-term success rather than chasing short-term targets. I think if he had known in detail the expected culture shifts up front, he would have survived.

The cultural shift is immediate and absolute: precision and speed replace politics and narrative. It becomes a culture of efficiency at all costs.

Balancing Efficiency With Organizational Survival

It's hard to overstate the need for balance when it comes to efficiency and cost cuts. Sometimes they're extremely significant and must be done. I've been in a situation where we cut 10% of our white-collar workforce and executed it in a ninety-day period. That was required by the business for cash-flow purposes, not because there had been some great time study of workflows that resulted in 10% less headcount and 10% less work.

As a leadership team, the challenge is to manage the planning of that decision while also communicating it to the organization in such a way that they understand it's part of an overall strategy. They need to see that it makes sense and that it won't happen every quarter or necessarily every year. There's both art and science in shaping the right narrative—and it's vital to keep communicating it to the broader team through town halls and in-person meetings. When efficiency measures and cost cuts feel random, poorly planned, or lacking empathy, morale erodes, turnover rises, and top talent walks out the door.

Taking costs out of overhead structure and supply chain becomes imperative. When efficiency becomes dogma, cultural DNA gets rewritten in the service of margin. Talent turnover and a decline in morale follow. The solution is to translate financial goals into human systems so the team can win without burning out. Make sure the team understands what you're doing with efficiency, why it's necessary, and how it's actually being planned ahead of time and executed properly.

EFFICIENCY WITHOUT LIMITS

Efficiency is powerful—but without balance, it becomes self-defeating. Few stories illustrate this more vividly than Burger King under 3G Capital. The private equity firm's extreme discipline on cost, structure, and efficiency transformed Burger King into a financial powerhouse—but at the cost of cultural strain and long-term brand health.

In 2010, 3G Capital acquired Burger King for $3.3 billion, taking it private in one of the decade's most notable consumer LBOs. The firm immediately deployed its trademark zero-based budgeting (ZBB) model, a radical approach that requires every department to justify each expense annually from zero—rather than adjusting from the prior year's baseline. 3G also slashed SG&A, refranchised most company-owned restaurants, centralized procurement, and streamlined operations to create an asset-light, cash-generating business.

The results were striking. Profitability surged, margins expanded, and the company quickly became lean and efficient. Just two years later, in 2012, Burger King was relisted on the NYSE via a merger with Justice Holdings. By 2014, 3G merged Burger King with Tim Hortons to form Restaurant Brands International (RBI)—a publicly traded parent company that would later acquire Popeyes (2017) and Firehouse Subs (2021). The financial model scaled elegantly, positioning RBI as one of the world's largest quick-service restaurant groups.

Yet the success came with trade-offs. Inside the company, employee morale weakened as headcount cuts, aggressive performance monitoring, and rigid budget controls fostered a culture of pressure and turnover. Among franchisees, relations grew tense over mandated capital expenditures such as store remodels and digital system upgrades that didn't always translate to sales growth. Cost compression at the supply level sometimes squeezed franchise margins further, creating resentment within the network.

Operationally, the focus on budgeting precision also curbed innovation. With marketing spend tightly controlled and new product pipelines trimmed, Burger King occasionally fell behind McDonald's and Wendy's in menu innovation, advertising resonance, and digital adoption. In several markets, service quality and customer satisfaction declined as labor hours were minimized to meet cost targets. The brand's "flame-grilled" heritage and irreverent tone remained strong, but inconsistent execution began to dilute overall brand momentum.

In short, the same efficiency that boosted short-term returns also introduced long-term fragility. 3G's operational discipline produced remarkable financial performance, but it came at the expense of softer, slower-building assets—culture, franchise trust, and customer connection. Recognizing this, RBI in recent years has reinvested in marketing, technology, and menu innovation, particularly under its "Reclaim the Flame" plan launched in 2022, aimed at restoring Burger King's US competitiveness.

The takeaway is clear: efficiency must have limits. Lean operations drive short-term success, but enduring value requires reinvestment in people, innovation, and customer experience. Without a clear communication plan and a measured approach to cost discipline, efficiency risks becoming a blunt instrument—one that cuts into the brand equity and goodwill on which long-term success depends.

KEY CHAPTER TAKEAWAYS

1. Expect an Overnight Reset
- PE culture doesn't evolve slowly—it lands on day one with dashboards, KPIs, and exit math.
- Past performance or legacy culture won't shield you; only cash flow and EBITDA traction matter.

2. Learn the New Scoreboard Fast
- Survival depends on translating your story into numbers that PE tracks weekly and monthly.
- Build reporting infrastructure before they ask—don't scramble after the first Monday meeting.

3. Autonomy Vanishes Quickly
- Long-term workflows, narrative leadership, and politics collapse under daily and weekly oversight.
- Leaders who can't adapt to dashboard-driven management are quickly sidelined or replaced.

4. Anticipate the Reporting Avalanche
- PE demands immediate clarity on inventories, receivables, payables, and overhead levers.
- Pre-build systems for clean, timely data so you control the narrative instead of reacting to it.

5. Efficiency Cuts Need Balance
- Efficiency is inevitable, but random cuts create fear, turnover, and cultural collapse.
- Link cost cuts to a clear, strategic story and communicate them in person, not just via spreadsheet.

6. The CFO Becomes Your Navigator
- CFOs are the central translators of PE's financial lens into daily action.
- CEOs who partner closely with their CFO keep the board confident and pressure manageable.

7. Translate Finance into Human Terms
- Margin targets and zero-based budgeting must be connected to people, workflows, and survival.
- Leaders must actively manage morale, turnover, and franchisee and employee buy-in during the reset.

8. Efficiency Is a Double-Edged Sword
- Ruthless cost control (like 3G's Burger King model) creates near-term EBITDA lift.
- But without reinvestment in brand, people, and customer experience, long-term value erodes.

9. PE Has Unilateral Power
- With majority control, PE can change leadership, shift strategy, or restructure at will.
- Stay ahead with transparency, readiness, and credible alternatives for value levers.

10. Culture Fractures = Performance Fractures
- In compressed PE timelines, cultural misalignment or morale decay quickly hit the numbers.
- Protect culture by explaining the "why" of changes and aligning everyone to exit-driven priorities.

In a PE takeover, culture will change immediately, but performance pressure will last much longer. In the next chapter, we'll break down how PE firms force results and what it means for you, and how value creation becomes a spreadsheet mandate.

CHAPTER 10

Value or Bust—How PE Firms Force Performance in Portfolio Companies

I was part of a value-creation plan that looked good on the spreadsheet, but the cost cuts went way too far—undermining morale and eroding the brand.

In this chapter, you'll see how PE firms operationalize performance pressure from debt loads to weekly reporting and how to stay effective without being steamrolled.

The Value-Creation Gameplan: Getting Ahead Of PE Expectations

It is imperative to actively get ahead of and manage the value-or-bust agenda of the PE firm ahead of time. That requires extensive planning and communication to the organization.

Create an aggressive plan that caters to what the PE firm wants and needs: spreadsheets and numbers, key metrics on reporting around EBITDA, cash flow, detailed financials, and other metrics. Create detailed planning on reductions in corporate and supply chain overhead and cost of goods with clear targets and clear timings. Develop the game plan for real estate and asset sales and leasebacks. Manage inventories, accounts receivable, and accounts payable to maximize cash. All these things can be planned out, rigorously embraced as strategies, and then executed, tracked, and reported on a timely basis.

It's far better to get ahead of the process than to have the PE firm drive it down from above—their way is often burdensome, less human, and far harder to implement. Getting on top of this will decrease stress for your team, lower friction, and enable better communication, all of which will increase their effectiveness.

When The Numbers Don't Add Up: The Performance Pressure Cooker

The first thing that happens in the performance cycle is spreadsheet overload. Performance becomes a numbers game. Free cash flow and adjusted EBITDA drive every decision, pushing softer strategies to the sidelines. When numbers miss stated targets, the human costs ramp up: layoffs, strategy pivots, asset sales, and leadership churn.

One of the core pressures in PE is that once numbers and targets are set, missing them—even briefly—creates immediate tension and intense action to get back on track. Some of the reasons for the miss may be external. Maybe the market itself has slowed down faster than expected, or there's been a change in taxes or regulatory situation, resulting in lower performance numbers in the spreadsheets than expected. That doesn't really matter to the PE firm. What matters most is getting back on track. That often means incremental cost cuts, asset sales or sale-leasebacks, pressure to lift underlying performance, stronger sales, and improved margins to cover forecast shortfalls.

Anchor your strategy in the financials but translate them into people-aligned execution. It's essential to translate spreadsheet management into clear communication—explaining the numbers in a way the organization understands, while keeping morale high.

I helped run a value-creation plan that checked every box but tanked morale and weakened the brand. Because of external factors (increase in tariffs in one of our major markets and massive increase in costs because of supply chain issues with Covid), we found ourselves fighting a battle on multiple fronts while trying to hit numbers that had become unrealistic overnight. Our performance tanked. We faced lower sales and shrinking margins. We were also trapped in a price-inelastic market with a highly substitutable product. We couldn't raise prices without losing customers, so we had to slash costs far beyond our original plan: massive overhead cuts, supply chain reductions, and asset sales that nobody saw coming.

The strategy pivot created chaos. Morale plummeted as employees watched us cut headcount and sell off assets they considered valuable. Marketing budgets disappeared, brand investment evaporated, and managing through it felt like steering a ship in a hurricane. In situations like this, all you can do is overcommunicate relentlessly. Make people understand why the plan changed, why these cuts are necessary, and how, if we execute quickly and efficiently, we might survive to see the market improve.

Numbers matter, but not at the expense of the narrative, especially when it comes to culture. You can drive numbers hard and miss the hidden damage to your brand, infrastructure, supply chain, production capabilities, and salesforce. The real danger lies in how incremental initiatives to drive value beyond the original plan can tax the organization's capability, morale, and long-term brand value. You constantly face decisions about this balance, knowing you must find ways to reinvest in the brand and infrastructure at the right time while communicating effectively to counterbalance the negatives.

The Reporting Gauntlet: Surviving Data Demands

Then comes the reporting gauntlet. Weekly reports become the new heartbeat, and your survival depends on how well you pulse back. Leaders face constant scrutiny through real-time metrics and performance dashboards. When forecasts are missed, reporting demands intensify and decision-making shifts toward strict command and control. I've seen monthly financial and operational reporting decks that reach upward of three hundred slides. This is too much detail for any one person to read every month.

The way to get around this is to manage it proactively and get ahead of it. Boil down to the basics of what the PE firm needs to help manage the business. When forecasts are missed and EBITDA and cash flow head in the wrong direction, exit timelines start to delay. It's a natural human tendency to expand reporting and require even more tracking to make everyone feel better about being off forecast or missing original exit timing. This needs careful management because it can freeze an organization with non-value-adding activity and prevent execution of the value levers that actually improve EBITDA and cash flow.

If you miss too many targets, you risk immediate restructuring or exit. Build reporting systems that show progress and anticipate variances before they bite you. You're managing the story, not just reacting to it. And never forget EBITDA and cash flow. You can build effective, proactive systems if you get ahead of it and simplify reporting to focus on what drives these key metrics (sales margins, cost-reduction initiatives, supply chain improvements, cost of goods, inventories, accounts payable, and receivable changes). Once you gain the trust of your PE firm by delivering the data they need on a timely basis, you can reduce reporting requirements over time.

I once watched finance executives who couldn't keep up with the cadence and mounting targets get replaced. I've seen this in several PE-backed firms: when performance doesn't happen, reporting requirements multiply, spreadsheet demands increase, and pressure builds on the CFO and the team. A company can reach a breaking point where the CFO focuses solely on meeting reporting requirements instead of driving asset sales, cash generation projects, cost-reduction initiatives, and business planning. That's when you know the system has broken down completely.

Burnout becomes inevitable when CFOs find themselves drowning under impossible demands. Sometimes private equity firms mistake this overload for underperformance and replace perfectly capable executives who are simply stretched beyond human limits. In high-pressure moments, visibility equals credibility. Leaders who fail to show how they're managing the strain often pay for it with their jobs.

The Mirage Of Value Creation: When Short-Term Wins Become Long-Term Disasters

The pressure inherent in private equity creates dangerous territory in which value creation can transform into a myth, and then excessive performance management drives companies past their breaking point. Not all value-creation strategies actually create real long-term value; some merely shift it around or extract it entirely, leaving companies hollowed out.

Private equity firms deploy numerous tactics that can devastate company strength long-term. They slash people and capabilities that drive differentiated customer experiences. Marketing budgets for brand-building get gutted. Strategic assets that aren't immediately critical but add substantial long-term value get sold off. Companies find themselves selling and leasing back their own real estate just to generate cash flow (sometimes creating less competitive, higher long-term cost structures). Each move might look smart on paper, but the cumulative effect can be catastrophic.

The real danger emerges when these tactics create unsustainable numbers. I've witnessed initiatives that produce adjusted EBITDA figures that look impressive to potential buyers but rest on quicksand. The marketing investment will need to return eventually. Digital and selling capabilities will require rebuilding. Lease payments exceed what depreciation and asset ownership would have cost. The sustainability isn't there long-term.

What you're left with is financial theater designed to inflate exit multiples. The next purchaser ends up paying 20% to 40% more than the company is actually worth, discovering too late that they've bought a mirage. This creates an even more high-pressure environment for the subsequent private equity cycle, as the new owners desperately try to justify their inflated purchase price.

The result becomes a vicious cycle that can destroy companies entirely, spinning through ownership after ownership until someone finally calls for a complete reset—if the company survives that long.

Sustainable Value Vs. Financial Theater

These moves can reduce real operating strength, creating exit optics without a resilience balance. In this context, it's better to balance short-term levers with sustainable levers: customer lifetime value, operations maturity, and strategic hires. Ensure your company keeps the capabilities to drive growth, avoids cutting essentials that must later be replaced, invests in marketing and brand at or above industry norms, and maintains the strategic assets needed for long-term success.

When all that is in place, your EBITDA is strong and sustainable. That will lead to a better exit and a better company outcome later. With the next owner, real value will survive scrutiny and cycles.

BUSINESS CASE

EXCESSIVE COST-CUTTING AFFECTING THE CUSTOMER EXPERIENCE

Sears is a cautionary tale of how financial engineering and relentless cost-cutting—tactics often borrowed from private equity playbooks—can strip a legacy retailer of its vitality. The company's slow-motion collapse illustrates how a focus on cost-cutting and asset monetization, without reinvestment in the customer experience, can erode brand equity beyond repair.

In 2005, hedge fund ESL Investments, led by Eddie Lampert, orchestrated the $11 billion merger of Sears, Roebuck & Co., and Kmart, creating Sears Holdings Corporation. The merger

---

was initially hailed as a bold turnaround strategy—a chance to combine two struggling icons into a leaner, more competitive retail platform. But Lampert's playbook leaned heavily on financial engineering rather than operational renewal. Instead of modernizing stores, building a digital platform, or reinvigorating merchandising, Sears embarked on aggressive cost-cutting and real estate monetization.

Hundreds of owned properties were spun off or sold, including to a real estate investment trust Lampert created in 2015 called Seritage Growth Properties, which purchased about 235 Sears and Kmart stores for $2.7 billion. Those stores were then leased back to Sears, turning owned assets into recurring rent liabilities. In the short term, these moves generated liquidity and created the appearance of profitability. In the long term, they hollowed out the retailer's operational flexibility and left stores increasingly run-down, understaffed, and outdated.

Meanwhile, Sears lagged badly in e-commerce and digital integration as Amazon, Walmart, and Target invested aggressively in technology, data analytics, and omnichannel capabilities. The focus on cutting SG&A and squeezing inventory costs led to empty shelves, slow restocking, and poor in-store service—all of which alienated customers. Once-loyal shoppers migrated elsewhere, and vendor relationships deteriorated as payments slowed and credit tightened.

The consequences were stark. From more than 3,500 Sears and Kmart stores in 2005, the company's footprint shrank to fewer than 700 locations by 2017. Following its Chapter 11 bankruptcy filing in 2018, only about 200 stores remained open.

The drawn-out decline resulted in the loss of over 250,000 jobs across the United States and left once-vibrant malls and communities with vacant anchor spaces.

Ultimately, Sears was transformed from a retailer into a financial experiment—one that prioritized short-term liquidity events over customer engagement and brand renewal. The company's once-dominant position in American retail was squandered through asset stripping, deferred reinvestment, and cost-driven austerity.

The broader lesson: efficiency without reinvestment is unsustainable. Financial engineering can mask deterioration temporarily, but in consumer-facing sectors where loyalty and experience drive repeat business, the results are devastating when capital extraction replaces innovation. Sears demonstrates that you can't spreadsheet your way out of structural decline—and that focusing on balance-sheet optics at the expense of the customer ultimately destroys long-term enterprise value.

The Harsh Reality of PE Ownership

Most of the insight you need as an operator or an investor regarding PE ownership can be gathered by answering two fundamental questions:

1. Are we building lasting enterprise value, or are we simply dressing up short-term numbers?
2. Do our performance metrics support healthy, sustainable execution?

Push for value levers that outlast the exit before cost cuts and debt deals box you in. When forecasts miss expectations, PE firms instinctively tighten control and double down on reporting requirements. Plan for that moment before it happens—the spreadsheet doesn't reveal burnout until it's too late.

PE firms deploy leverage extensively across their portfolio companies, typically using 50% to 70% debt in the total capital structure. This compares to roughly 30% for public companies. In this high-leverage environment, cash flow and EBITDA become the only metrics that matter. Underperformance in these areas versus expectations can create a survival crisis and therefore can trigger brutal intervention and frequently drastic action.

During crisis moments, PE firms abandon softer management strategies and focus exclusively on spreadsheets and numbers. They rely heavily on operational improvements, often bringing in external operating partners and consultants to execute rapid changes. The playbook is predictable: most value gets created through leverage, cost cuts, and working capital management (inventory, receivables, payables). Real estate sales and leasebacks also play a surprisingly large role in value creation across many portfolio companies. In most deals, a smaller portion of the value creation is then realized by process improvements, IT upgrades, brand investments, and strategic people investments.

M&A rollups and standardization can sometimes drive significant value creation, but only if you avoid overpaying, a mistake that kills some deals more than any operational misstep. The sobering truth about PE value creation is that on average more than 50% comes from leverage and multiple expansion, not operational excellence. The remainder flows primarily from cost reduction, operational improvements, and real estate transactions, with organic growth contributing the smallest portion.

When actual results fall significantly short of forecasts, the PE playbook becomes ruthlessly predictable: delayed exit timelines, aggressive cost-cutting, more asset divestitures, and management changes. Even worse, it can end up in financial restructuring or bankruptcy.

In addition to all this, hidden cost burdens often catch management teams off guard. PE firm fees and transaction support costs like legal, consultants, and PR can run significantly higher than anticipated and devour meaningful portions of portfolio-company profits. These costs can also appear hypocritical to portfolio-company employees, who are often being asked to make drastic cost cuts and scale back needed investments at the same time. The single advantage private companies maintain over public ones is dramatically lower regulatory compliance and reporting costs.

That said, PE firms differ sharply in how they approach value creation. Some—like Warburg Pincus, Carlyle, and Wind Point Partners—tend to emphasize revenue growth and brand investment in a more balanced fashion. Others—such as Bain Capital, TPG, and 3G Capital—are associated with higher leverage and more significant cost-cutting. Before you decide to work with, sell to, or invest in a firm, make sure you understand which approach they follow.

VALUE CREATION THROUGH BRAND-BUILDING AND GLOBAL EXPANSION

Carlyle's acquisition of Golden Goose Deluxe Brand is a compelling example of private equity value creation via accelerating brand momentum, international expansion, and channel transformation. It demonstrates how a distinctive brand with stylistic authenticity can be scaled globally, provided the right capital, operational support, and discipline are applied.

In 2017, Carlyle acquired 100% of Golden Goose from Ergon Capital Partners and other shareholders in a deal reportedly valuing the business at roughly €400 million. At the time, Golden Goose was a fast-growing Italian luxury-casual brand, best known for its distressed-style sneakers and distinctive aesthetic, with modest direct retail operations and a strong presence in wholesale and franchise distribution.

From the beginning, Carlyle's strategy was to preserve the brand's unique DNA while scaling the infrastructure needed to compete globally. Partnering closely with CEO Silvio Campara, Carlyle invested in digital capabilities and e-commerce, expanded flagship retail presence, and optimized the wholesale network. Over the partnership, the brand grew from about seven directly operated stores to nearly a hundred, and its direct-to-consumer share rose from ~10% to around 45%. Meanwhile, Golden Goose's EBITDA doubled, moving from

~€32 million in 2016 to ~€83 million by 2019—reflecting compound EBITDA growth rates in the high 30s (%) annually.

Carlyle was mindful to balance expansion with authenticity. Much of Golden Goose's supply chain and craftsmanship remained rooted in Italy, preserving its heritage appeal even as the brand pushed into the US, China, Japan, and other aspirational luxury markets. Product diversification (beyond sneakers into apparel, accessories, new footwear categories) also helped broaden relevance beyond a seasonal or niche base. The firm used its global network to accelerate entry into luxury retail hubs and coordinated marketing efforts (celebrity placements, selective store placements) to lift brand prestige.

In 2020, Carlyle exited its majority stake to Permira, while retaining a minority investment, marking a successful realization of the value created. During its stewardship, Golden Goose more than doubled its revenues, significantly expanded profitability, and elevated its positioning in the global luxury sneaker/lifestyle space.

Key lessons and takeaways from Carlyle's Golden Goose investment include:

Brand distinctiveness is a growth lever—When a brand has a unique aesthetic or emotional resonance, capital and operational support can help amplify that rather than homogenize it.

Channel transformation is critical—Moving aggressively into direct-to-consumer (digital + flagship retail) can shift margin architecture and narrative control.

Scale must respect craft and heritage—Rapid expansion should not erode the authenticity that gives luxury its justification; balance is key.

Operational and management strengthening matter—Scaling a creative brand globally requires stronger corporate governance, systems, and talent alongside creative leadership.

Exit timing and multiple expansion—The transformation must align with favorable market conditions; Carlyle's exit to Permira captured a premium valuation as the market recognized luxury streetwear momentum.

Carlyle's work with Golden Goose stands in contrast to extractive buyouts. It is a case where patient capital, aligned incentives, and strategic brand support drove durable value—not just financial engineering.

DEEP DIVE

HOW PRIVATE EQUITY FIRMS CUT COSTS

Cost-cutting is one of the oldest and most reliable levers in the private equity playbook. From the moment a deal closes, PE firms typically set aggressive cost targets that management is expected to hit. These targets aren't vague aspirations—they're built into the deal model and tied directly to the exit strategy. If the model assumes a 20% EBITDA improvement, leadership knows from day one that cost reductions must deliver a major part of that lift.

The first area most firms attack is general overhead. Corporate functions like HR, finance, legal, and IT are prime candidates for consolidation or outsourcing. Duplicate roles are eliminated, back-office processes are centralized, and discretionary spending is slashed. At the same time, firms scrutinize travel budgets, headcount, and vendor contracts—any area where costs can be standardized across the portfolio.

Another major lever is the supply chain. PE firms often bring in procurement specialists or outside consultants to renegotiate supplier contracts, consolidate vendors, and apply purchasing power across multiple portfolio companies. This can deliver significant savings quickly, but it often comes at the cost of long-standing supplier relationships. Inventory management is also tightened, with firms pushing for leaner operations and faster turnover of working capital.

Many firms deploy zero-based budgeting (ZBB) as a discipline. Instead of rolling forward last year's budget with incremental changes, ZBB requires every cost to be justified from scratch each year. Nothing is assumed. Marketing spend, travel, and even office supplies have to be defended line by line. This process can feel painful for management, but it forces discipline and helps surface areas of hidden inefficiency.

To make sure targets are realistic—and to hold management accountable—firms rely heavily on benchmarking and external consultants. Benchmarks compare company performance against industry peers, providing a data-driven case for why certain cuts are "achievable." Outside consultants are often brought in early to map opportunities, validate targets, and push management to move faster than they would on their own. These consultants serve as both a hammer and a shield: management gets the hammer of pressure to deliver, while the PE firm gets the shield by making the consultants deliver the analysis and recommendations.

Perhaps the biggest difference from similar exercises in public companies is the timeline. In public firms, cost-reduction programs often roll out over two to three years, with plenty of room for delays, internal politics, and incremental progress. In PE-backed companies, the window is much tighter—cost savings are expected to show up within the first twelve months, sometimes faster. Management teams are given little room for excuses or delays, because the fund's exit clock is already ticking. That compressed timeline can feel brutal, but it also explains why PE-driven cost-cutting often delivers results much quicker than comparable public-company initiatives.

The end result is a rapid and often dramatic cost reduction. For some businesses, this discipline unlocks real efficiency and sharper operations. For others, the cuts can feel short-sighted, while draining talent, damaging culture, or undermining long-term growth. But from the PE firm's perspective, cost reduction is one of the few levers that can be reliably controlled and timed to fit an exit window—which is why it remains a cornerstone of the model.

KEY CHAPTER TAKEAWAYS

1. Get Ahead of the Playbook
- Build your own value-creation plan before PE imposes theirs.
- Anchor it in cash flow, EBITDA, and timely, transparent reporting.

2. Numbers Rule, Narrative Guides
- PE pressure is relentless when forecasts miss; the fix is always more cuts, more asset sales, more reporting.
- Leaders survive by translating spreadsheets into stories people understand.

3. Expect Spreadsheet Overload
- Missed targets trigger reporting bloat—300-slide decks that freeze execution.
- Simplify: track only the levers that really move EBITDA and cash flow.

4. When Pressure Mounts, People Pay
- Shortfalls lead to layoffs, pivots, and leadership churn.
- The best executives overcommunicate why painful moves are happening and protect morale where possible.

5. Financial Theater Is a Trap
- Adjusted EBITDA tricks and asset sales create optics, not endurance.
- Short-term wins without reinvestment will hollow out brand, talent, and operations.

6. Cost-Cutting Is the First Lever
- Overhead, supply chain, and zero-based budgeting are standard early moves.

- Unlike public companies, PE expects savings within six to twelve months, not over several years.

7. Balance Efficiency With Resilience
- Real value comes from combining financial discipline with reinvestment in brand, people, and tech.
- Ignore this balance, and you risk becoming the next Sears cautionary tale.

8. Leverage Shapes Everything
- PE capital structures often run at 50%–70% debt versus ~30% for public firms.
- That debt makes EBITDA and cash flow into survival metrics, not just performance indicators.

9. Plan for Hidden Costs
- PE ownership layers on fees, consultants, and transaction charges.
- Budget for these upfront so they don't silently erode profitability.

10. Know What Really Drives Returns
- Over half of PE value creation comes from leverage and multiple expansion, not operational genius.
- Set expectations accordingly: don't mistake the model's math for long-term operational excellence.

Performance pressure is inevitable, but the way you respond determines whether you build something enduring or just polish the optics. The next chapter will expose how to position for a strong exit without sacrificing the core of what you built.

CHAPTER 11

Exit Like a Pro—3 Factors that Make or Break Your Deal

I was involved in an exit that got delayed too long, and watched the valuation drop as market conditions turned.

In this chapter, you'll learn why PE exits are less about milestones and more about momentum. You'll also learn how timing precision, narrative control, and strategic guts determine the final outcome. These three elements are deeply interconnected—each influencing the others in ways that can ultimately make or break an exit.

The Interconnected Dynamics Of Exit Success

Let's start with narrative, something that begins from day one of private equity ownership and gets crafted and stress-tested as you progress. By definition, narrative needs evidence to create value. This is where timing becomes critical: when do you get the evidence to create the right timing that supports the narrative for an exit? How can you measure that you are incrementally building the evidence along the way?

On top of this, external factors can devastate timing. If you're pursuing an IPO and market conditions suddenly deteriorate, you might have to wait an additional year or two. Maybe some of the evidence in your narrative starts to disintegrate while you're waiting. This is where nerve comes in. Sometimes you have to go ahead and exit even though the timing isn't perfect, because you know the evidence in your narrative won't be as strong if you wait too long. Or you have to wait longer, and massive anticipation and pressure builds as external market factors and timing gradually improve. The decision to wait takes enormous nerve, because you're still under pressure and you've got to keep the balance together.

To exit like a pro, thinking about and planning ahead on narrative, timing, and nerve—building this resilience—is everything.

Timing As The Ultimate Value Multiplier

The real value multiple for a successful exit is timing. Even strong businesses lose value in mistimed exits. PE firms obsess over exit windows because small shifts in rates, sentiment, or sector news can shrink valuations. Wait too long and the story gets stale, performance softens, or macro shifts undercut gains. And time is money. Every year can reduce the overall deal IRR significantly.

To manage exit timing, plan the exit strategy early and build options that flex with market signals. Be in a position where you have several exit options, and you can follow through with one of them at the right time based on macroeconomic favorability and company performance.

I have seen valuation drop because leadership hesitated to exit before conditions changed and they didn't have multiple exit options. In this specific situation, the first two years in the deal were extremely lucrative. We had reached what might be looked at as a base-level exit—not the kind of lucrative exit we really wanted, but at least something where we had made real progress in the company and there was an opportunity to exit. We had no reason to believe that the next three years would be so difficult because things were going well. Then there were significant external market issues, both regulatory and macroeconomic. The company's momentum was lost, and the ability to exit in the way that we wanted to was also lost.

The takeaway here is that sometimes timing can be unlucky. Other times, the timing might not be exactly when you want, but you must always have your eye on the exit and understand the risks and potential opportunities of the moment. Exits reward agility, not perfection.

BUSINESS CASE

TIMING IS EVERYTHING (AND PATIENCE HELPS)

Few deals better illustrate the power of patience and strategic discipline in private equity than Blackstone's acquisition of Hilton Hotels. What began as one of the boldest—and riskiest—leveraged buyouts in history became one of the industry's most profitable exits.

In July 2007, just before the global financial crisis, The Blackstone Group acquired Hilton Hotels Corporation for approximately $26 billion, including over $20 billion in debt. The timing could not have been worse: within months, the

2008 financial crisis brought global travel to a standstill. Hotel occupancy rates plunged, credit markets froze, and Hilton's debt-heavy capital structure appeared unsustainable. Many analysts predicted that Blackstone's record-setting LBO would end in bankruptcy.

Instead, Blackstone chose patience over panic. The firm worked closely with Hilton's management to restructure the company's debt, negotiating with a very large number of lenders to extend maturities and reduce interest burdens. In 2010, Blackstone successfully refinanced $20 billion in debt, injecting roughly $800 million of additional equity to stabilize operations. These moves bought Hilton critical time to focus on long-term transformation rather than short-term survival.

The turnaround centered on operational modernization and a strategic shift to an "asset-light" model. Under Blackstone's ownership, Hilton accelerated its move away from owning hotels toward franchising and management contracts, a model that produced higher-margin, fee-based revenue with lower capital intensity. The firm also invested heavily in technology and loyalty infrastructure, enhancing Hilton's central reservation systems and expanding the Hilton Honors program, which grew to become one of the most powerful customer ecosystems in global hospitality.

At the same time, Hilton pursued international expansion, particularly in China, the Middle East, and Latin America, where branded hotel demand was booming. With Blackstone's capital and relationships, Hilton doubled its global footprint, adding more than a thousand new hotels during its private ownership period. The company also revitalized its brand portfolio, expanding from nine to over a dozen brands, including Curio, Home2 Suites, and Tru by Hilton, enabling it to capture both budget and luxury travelers.

By the time Hilton returned to the public markets in December 2013, the transformation was complete. The IPO valued Hilton at more than $19 billion, and the company's market capitalization continued to rise as investors rewarded its efficient, high-return business model. Blackstone began selling down its stake gradually, completing its full exit in 2018. The result: more than $14 billion in profits on an initial six-billion-dollar equity investment, making it one of the most successful private equity deals ever executed.

The Hilton case underscores that timing sets the challenge, but execution determines the outcome. Blackstone's patience through crisis—combined with operational upgrades, global expansion, and technological reinvestment—turned a near-disaster into a masterclass in long-term value creation. It also redefined how private equity approaches the hospitality sector: as a platform for brand, data, and systems scale, not just asset ownership.

The broader lesson is clear: discipline, alignment, and time horizon matter as much as deal size. In private equity, survival through downturns often defines the best returns. Hilton's story proves that patient capital, when paired with strategic reinvention, can turn even the worst market timing into record-breaking success.

The Narrative Machine: Selling The Story Behind The Numbers

The second part of exit that's as important as timing is the narrative machine. Buyers don't just buy cash flow; they buy the story. There's always an opportunity to change the narrative or explain it in a way that makes future value more evident or clear.

The Blackstone/Hilton case study is an extreme example where a company has a lot of issues and is bleeding money. Blackstone flipped the script on each issue by showing how much better the situation would be in the future. You're asking people to invest hard-earned dollars at a much higher valuation based on that promise. But there are plenty of short-term cases where overinvestment in brand or infrastructure has led to lower margins or reduced EBITDA and cash flow.

The question becomes: Is there a way to evidence an exit through narrative crafting that convinces investors that the future is much brighter than current financials suggest? Exit decks often drive value as much as spreadsheets, especially when growth narratives shift risk perception. If your narrative doesn't match the market appetite, you lose leverage or walk away with less.

The exit arc must be designed early—while the deal is still being finalized and the new portfolio company is taking shape. The narrative should begin during due diligence: start crafting the exit story and how it will resonate in the market. Then, stress-test it continuously with external perspectives to refine and strengthen it.

Carefully consider what would be an exit narrative across multiple exit options. Maintain optionality on multiple scenarios: IPO, selling to the trade, selling to another PE firm, or a continuation fund. Maybe one or two elements of the narrative stay the same, and maybe one or two have optionality for different outcomes. The quicker you get a narrative that matches your key value creation levers and where you're going to be when you exit, the better. The more you can stress-test your narrative against market peers, future scenarios, your PE partner, and outside investors, the more likely it is to hold up through an exit.

TURNING POOR FINANCIAL RESULTS INTO A STRONG NARRATIVE

Uber offers a telling example of how the right exit narrative can shape success, even in a tough operating environment. Uber's pre-IPO adjustments weren't just financial fine-tuning. They were narrative engineering—a deliberate attempt to reframe operational and financial chaos into a story investors could believe in. The Uber case underscores how critical the exit narrative is in private equity and venture-backed deals. Numbers alone don't secure capital. The story does.

In 2017–2018, Uber was facing mounting losses, public governance controversies, management turnover, and relentless competition from Lyft in the US and from local champions in key international markets. The financials told a bleak story: billions in annual operating losses, cash burn from subsidized rides, and no clear timeline to profitability. Yet instead of leading with those numbers, Uber's team—guided by new CEO Dara Khosrowshahi and its investors—recast the narrative around inevitability and scale. The message was not about where Uber was at the moment, but about where it was destined to go.

The company's IPO story leaned heavily on platform potential and global mobility dominance. Uber positioned itself as more than a ride-hailing app: it was the foundation for a global transportation and logistics ecosystem, a category-defining player in personal mobility, food delivery, freight, and even autonomous vehicles. The narrative emphasized network effects—with 91 million monthly active platform users generating billions of trips annually, investors were reminded that competitors couldn't easily replicate Uber's scale.

Uber buttressed this story with selective but powerful metrics. Net revenue almost tripled from $3.8 billion in 2016 to $11.3 billion in 2018, showing rapid top-line expansion even as losses widened. The company highlighted its geographic breadth— operating in over seven hundred cities across sixty-three countries—to reinforce the idea that Uber was not a US story but a global platform with optionality. By reframing its financials within the narrative of "growth now, dominance later," Uber gave investors a reason to see losses as strategic investments rather than structural failures.

The lesson here is that exit narrative is a form of value creation in itself. For Uber's backers, the IPO was a test of confidence: investors had to buy into the story of Uber's inevitability, not its short-term profitability. Crafting that story required aligning operations and metrics around a central theme, stress-testing the messaging against likely critiques (competition, regulatory risk, path to profit), and consistently projecting the company's future as larger than its current struggles. In May 2019, Uber raised $8.1 billion in its IPO at a 75.5-billion-dollar valuation—despite reporting a three-billion-dollar operating loss the year before.

Uber illustrates that numbers and narrative must work together. Poor results don't doom an exit if the story reframes those results as part of a credible long-term trajectory. Investors buy into the vision, not just the income statement. And in high-growth or disruptive industries, the ability to engineer and hold that narrative can mean the difference between a failed IPO and one of the largest listings in history.

Exit is theater and you're the director. Your ability to craft a narrative that fits the picture and resonates with investors—public, trade, or private equity—determines how well the story connects, much like a great movie. Your ability to paint the future for them and excite and delight will increase the value in your exit. And yes, don't forget the evidence built into an exciting trailer.

The Nerve Factor: Maintaining Discipline When Plans Derail

The third part of the exit that's so important is the nerve factor. The exit plan rarely survives first contact with the market. One of the key lessons in PE is that your diligence, valuation, investment thesis, business plan, and exit strategy will all eventually prove wrong. Execution of the plan never goes exactly as planned. Exits usually take longer than expected—only in rare cases do they happen sooner. More often, unforeseen challenges arise that demand resilience, constant replanning, and retiming from the team.

That requires confidence, nerve, and resilience. If those qualities are in place—and the value remains intact—a delayed exit can still be highly lucrative. PE teams must be able to adapt mid-exit to delays, down rounds, or strategic pivots. Emotional attachment or fear often lead to poor decisions, like holding too long or selling too quickly at a discount.

Make sure you maintain disciplined optionality. Know your walkaway terms, but keep momentum. Maintain your eye on the exit, the narrative, and the timing. Flexibility in exit planning is critical. An alternative path—like a private sale in year four instead of an IPO in year five—can often deliver greater value. It may still be below what the original expectation was, but the timing is right.

External markets can shift quickly. When conditions are strong—IPOs active, PE-to-PE sales robust, secondaries thriving, and fundraising buoyant—stay alert. Even if you're not fully ready to exit, those windows of opportunity may be the right time to act. Because these things all run in cycles, market conditions may change drastically within six, twelve, or eighteen months. Then you can find yourself stuck for another two or three years. That's why it's essential to weigh external market conditions just as carefully as your internal progress—EBITDA growth, cash flow improvement, and the strength of your narrative.

Calm doesn't mean stalling. It means control.

WHEN NARRATIVE AND TIMING CONVERGE

A standout business case shows how managing exit timing can be a powerful driver of value creation. By timing its IPO to coincide with peak public-market valuations—just before tech volatility set in—Warburg Pincus secured substantial gains and demonstrated the impact of strategic exit timing.

In 2014, the firm invested $100 million into Avalara, then a fast-growing but still niche provider of automated sales tax compliance software. The strategy went beyond capital injection. They guided Avalara through targeted acquisitions to broaden its product portfolio, expanded international capabilities to capture cross-border e-commerce growth, and repositioned the company to win larger enterprise contracts while deepening integrations with major ERP and e-commerce platforms (ERP is Enterprise Resource Planning, or an integrated software system to run core business processes).

Warburg Pincus helped accelerate scale and predictability by building recurring software-as-a-service revenue streams and strengthening channel partnerships.

When Avalara went public in 2018, the business had transformed into a category leader with global reach and strong market defensibility. After the IPO, Warburg Pincus began selling down its stake, completing its exit in 2019. It capitalized on robust valuation multiples in the public markets and realized a strong return even as broader tech sentiment was becoming more volatile.

A great exit isn't just when the market is hot; it's when your story makes it feel hotter. This happens when you align your exit narrative with broader themes like compliance, automation, and regulation to maximize strategic value.

Warburg Pincus exited Avalara at a strategic high despite tech market uncertainty. They crafted a compelling growth story around compliance tech, framed Avalara as essential infrastructure, and realized substantial returns. The key in this business case is that they took a somewhat fragmented business, scaled it, and turned it into significant software-as-a-service revenue. One of the big plays with PE is this concept of recurring monthly revenue. Software-as-a-service (SaaS) fits this model because it relies on renewable annual contracts that effectively guarantee ongoing revenue. In essence, it's a recurring revenue stream. They built and scaled these services as an infrastructure play with strong, predictable recurring cash flows. Then they timed the market perfectly, recognizing favorable conditions and aligning their exit accordingly. Everything came together for an exceptionally lucrative exit within three to four years, remarkably fast for this type of deal.

Without a tailored narrative and decisive timing, the deal could have been delayed or discounted as the software service market cooled. Avalara's PE owners used narrative timing, not just numbers, to shape buyer urgency and drive pace. If your story numbers, to shape buyer urgency and drive pace. If your story makes the exit feel hotter, but conditions outside are horrible, the exit may not work. When the market is hot and your narrative is extremely strong, it's almost exponential. It's one plus one equals three. That is the time to strike, even if it's slightly premature to your narrative or your performance based on what you're trying to achieve in terms of EBITDA and cash flow.

HOW PRIVATE EQUITY FIRMS EXIT A DEAL

When a private equity firm has owned a company for several years and created value, the question becomes: when and how do they exit? As we know, exiting is just as carefully planned as buying. The firm has to weigh timing—whether the market is hot, how the company is performing, and what buyers are out there. The decision isn't just about selling at the highest possible price; it's about ensuring a smooth transfer and delivering strong returns to the firm's investors. Much like the entry process, the exit relies on outside advisors, valuation work, legal agreements, and negotiations that mirror what happened when the company was first acquired.

Deciding When to Exit—Timing is critical. A firm looks at the company's growth curve, its ability to keep delivering results, and broader market conditions. If the company has hit key mile-stones—new products launched, profitability improved, debt paid down—it may be time to sell. The firm also looks outward: are competitors trading at high valuations? Are strategic buyers hungry for acquisitions? Is the IPO window open? Exiting too early might leave money on the table, but waiting too long can expose the firm to downturns or increased competition. Investment Committees review exit readiness and weigh scenarios against the fund's life cycle and investor expectations.

Exit Options—Private equity firms typically have five main exit routes:

1. Sale to a Strategic Buyer. This means selling to a company in the same industry that is looking for synergies—cost savings, cross-selling opportunities, or geographic expansion. Strategic buyers can often pay the highest price because they can justify it with these synergies.
2. Sale to Another PE Firm (Secondary Buyout). Here, one private equity firm sells to another, often because the company has grown but still has room for more transformation. The first firm realizes its returns, while the new owner sees a fresh runway for value creation.
3. Public Offering (IPO). If the company is large, well-known, and has a strong growth story, the firm may take it public. This route brings prestige and liquidity but also requires months of regulatory filings, underwriting banks, and careful investor roadshows. Sometimes firms only partially exit, keeping a stake even after listing.
4. Recapitalization. Another option is to refinance the company, taking on new debt and using it to return cash

to investors while still holding the equity. This isn't a full exit but can be a way to "take chips off the table" before a final sale.

5. Continuity Funds. In some cases, rather than selling to an outside buyer, a private equity firm may set up a new fund—often called a "continuation vehicle"—to acquire the company from its existing fund. This gives the original investors the choice of cashing out or rolling their investment into the new vehicle, while allowing the PE firm to stay invested in a business it believes has more room to grow. Continuity funds have become more common as firms seek flexibility when the timing isn't right for a traditional sale or IPO, but the company is performing well and warrants a longer runway.

Preparing the Company for Exit—Just as in an acquisition, preparation is everything. The firm works with advisors to prepare a detailed "equity story" that highlights growth, profitability, and transformation under private equity ownership. Accountants prepare audited financials, consultants help with market studies, and lawyers review contracts and liabilities. A confidential information memorandum (CIM) explaining the narrative and investment story is produced for potential buyers, and a data room is set up so bidders can conduct due diligence.

In many ways, the exit process mirrors the entry process. Potential buyers—whether corporates, other PE firms, or public investors—will bring in their own teams of advisors to scrutinize every detail. That means the seller's advisors must anticipate issues, prepare responses, and structure the deal to give confidence and maximize value.

Agreements and Advisors in the Exit Phase—The same groups of advisors that played a role in the acquisition are involved again on the sell side. Investment bankers run auctions, position the story, and drum up competitive tension. Lawyers negotiate the sale agreement, which looks strikingly similar to the purchase agreements used when buying, with reps and warranties, covenants, and closing conditions. Insurance brokers line up reps and warranties insurance if required. Tax specialists structure the sale to minimize leakage.

The mechanics are also familiar: exclusivity agreements, working capital adjustments, regulatory approvals, and closing funds flow. In many respects, it's the mirror image of Chapter 2's acquisition process—only now the private equity firm is the seller rather than the buyer.

Wrapping Up—In the end, the private equity exit process is about telling the story of value creation and convincing the next owner—whether a corporate buyer, another PE firm, or the public markets—that the company is worth the price. It requires the same discipline, the same coordination of advisors, and the same attention to detail as buying a company. By the time the deal closes, the firm has not only realized a return for its investors but also handed the company over to a new chapter of ownership. The baton passes once again—this time from seller to buyer—but the rhythm of the deal remains much the same.

PE EXITS BEYOND THE PLAYBOOK

When people think about private equity, they often imagine clean exits. You buy a company, improve it, and then sell it for a nice multiple to a strategic buyer or take it public. In reality, exits are rarely that straightforward. The classic IPO or sale to a bigger corporate still happens, but the exit environment today is far more complicated and often dictates how much money LPs and portfolio-company leaders actually see at the end of the deal.

One big shift is the rise of **secondary buyouts**. This is the act of selling a company not to a strategic (another firm in the industry) but to another PE fund. For years, this was considered a "last resort" exit, but now it's mainstream. Sometimes it makes sense: the next fund has a different thesis, more capital for rollups, or more patience on timing. Other times, it feels like musical chairs, with the same asset bouncing between funds until the music stops. If you're a management team, this can be frustrating—you find yourself doing another round of diligence, renegotiating your equity package, and starting over with new owners who may have a totally different playbook.

Another trend is the use of **continuation funds**. Instead of selling a company into the open market, the PE firm sets up a new vehicle and "sells" the asset to itself, inviting existing LPs to either cash out or roll their investment forward. For GPs, this solves the problem of being stuck in a weak exit market—it extends the hold period, keeps fees flowing, and avoids selling at a discount. For LPs, it's a tougher call: do you stay in with less liquidity or accept a valuation that might be below your expectations? For portfolio management, it often just means more uncertainty and longer timelines.

SPACs briefly offered another exit route, allowing PE firms to take companies public faster and with less scrutiny than a traditional IPO (SPACs means Special Purpose Acquisition Companies—basically public companies with no business that can buy private companies, thereby immediately making them public). While that market has cooled, it highlighted how creative PE firms have become when the traditional doors are closed. Some firms now even explore "evergreen" structures, where they hold assets longer-term and recycle capital, moving away from the rigid five-to-seven-year exit cycle.

The common thread in all of these exit mechanisms is that **exit timelines are getting longer and less predictable**. A deal that was modeled at five years may stretch to eight or even ten. That puts real strain on management teams who are often compensated with equity they can't touch until a sale. It also tests LP patience—capital is locked up longer, with fees still accruing. From the PE firm's perspective, the priority is to control timing, narrative, and structure to maximize value and keep returns looking steady.

KEY CHAPTER TAKEAWAYS

1. Timing Is the Real Multiple
- Small shifts in rates, sentiment, or sector news can compress valuation fast.
- Build an exit plan early with multiple doorways (trade, PE-to-PE, IPO, continuation fund) so you can move when the door opens.

2. Narrative, Nerve, Timing—A Linked System
- Narrative needs evidence, evidence needs timing, and imperfect timing requires nerve.
- Decide when to push ahead versus wait—before market drift erodes your story.

3. Craft the Exit Story on Day One
- Start shaping the equity story during diligence; align KPIs to prove it quarter by quarter.
- Stress-test the narrative with outsiders so it survives tough questions at sale.

4. Build Optionality, Not Hope
- Maintain parallel paths (banker outreach, strategic mapping, IPO prep) to avoid single-track risk.
- Keep live "plans B and C" with triggers that flip you between exit routes.

5. Evidence > Milestones
- Buyers pay for demonstrated traction (revenue growth, customer retention, mix, margin durability), not slick presentations.

- Stage proof points (pilot → scale → repeatability) to pace the exit clock.

6. Know When to Go (and When to Walk)
- Define go, no-go thresholds (valuation ranges, leverage caps, quality of bidders).
- Pre-agree walkaway terms so fear or greed doesn't trap you in a bad market.

7. Control the Process to Control the Price
- Pick bankers who fit your buyer universe and can create real competitive tension.
- Run a disciplined data room and CIM (Confidential Information Memorandum–the sellers pitch document) process; anticipate diligence landmines before buyers find them.

8. Keep Performance Hot During the Sale
- Exits die on flat quarters; protect your run-rate with a 180-day operating plan.
- Lock forecasting discipline; miss fewer, explain faster, fix sooner.

9. Use Structure as a Weapon
- Partial exits, earn-outs, and secondary/continuation vehicles can bridge timing gaps.
- Recaps de-risk early; don't let structure hide a weakening story—be transparent.

10. Lead the Humans, Not Just the KPIs
- Communicate the "why" to avoid employee morale slumps as scrutiny spikes during exit.
- Balance near-term optics with durable value—don't trade brand, talent, or tech for a prettier multiple.

You now understand the high-stakes dynamics of PE exits, but there's a quieter revolution underway, and it's already reshaping how private equity reaches your portfolio. Next, the surprising rise of retail investors in PE, including retirement plans and what you need to know to win.

PART III

WIN IN PE AS AN INVESTOR OR SELLER

"He that loveth silver shall not be satisfied with silver."

— ECCLESIASTES 5:10

CHAPTER 12

What Institutional and Retail Investors Wish They Knew Before Investing in PE

I have seen the unwind of a private equity fund and realized how little most people understood about liquidity, layered fees, waterfall structures, and capital drag.

In this chapter, you'll hear the cautionary truths investors face about committing to private equity and how to spot traps, decode terms, and protect your capital from the fine print. I will also include a solid framework for deciding how much of your portfolio to allocate to private assets and where to direct it. Let's dig down into what investors need to know about PE in four key areas: liquidity, returns, diversification, and investment cost.

The Four Pillars Of Private Equity Evaluation

Most PE investments are illiquid, and investors should plan on a ten-year investment horizon—longer than the three to five years often marketed. With capital increasingly coming from IRAs and 401(k)s, that horizon actually fits well, since retirement investors typically won't need withdrawals for at least a decade. In that sense, private equity's move into retirement accounts helps align the asset class with its natural liquidity profile.

Moreover, PE firms are trying to address this liquidity issue going forward. We're beginning to see new products that aren't tied to a single fund but instead rotate liquidity across funds. This structure provides periodic liquidity—greater flexibility than what a traditional PE fund can offer. In that case, a three-to-five-year horizon with some of these new products (which are called perpetual or evergreen funds because they go on indefinitely) may start to make sense. Read the fine print and understand it completely before you decide where to invest.

Second, we know that on average, returns for PE funds are 1%–2% higher over long periods of time than public-market indexes. That's not necessarily going to be the case in the future, but that's what the past indicates. Within that, just as we mentioned with active funds in other asset classes, there are winners and there are losers. It's important to understand the track record of the specific PE firm and fund offering that you're going to invest in order to try and get into that top quartile of quality.

Third, investing in PE provides broader diversification than investing solely in public markets. It expands your portfolio's exposure, and when returns are equal or better, that added diversification enhances overall performance over time. The key is understanding that during financial or economic crises, diversification tends to narrow—PE firms start behaving more like public markets. Yet over a five-to-ten-year horizon, those effects even out, and the diversification benefit remains strong.

Fourth, PE investing carries higher costs than public-market investing—especially when compared with low-cost passive index funds. It requires higher fees, higher carry interest, and higher costs across the board for PE general partners. Therefore, it is crucial to understand the hidden fees and net returns after fees for the specific PE firms and funds you're considering.

The Fee Fog Problem

The PE industry will hopefully address this as they develop retail products with lower costs and transparent fee structures, enabling investors to make informed decisions. For now, layers of fees and costs can obscure actual returns reported in PE. This is known as the fee fog. Gross returns might look impressive, but net returns are where wealth disappears—between management fees, carry interest, monitoring fees, and legal costs, investor returns can be drained long before exit. If you don't understand the full fee waterfall, you may celebrate on paper but lose in reality.

Returns should always be modeled net of fees, including fund-level and portfolio-level extractions. I've seen investors try to exit a fund, only to discover that fees had quietly eaten away far more value than they realized. Many PE firms don't report transparently—they bury layers of fees and costs within portfolio companies or treat them as separate one-offs. This will improve as PE funds prepare for retail IRAs and 401(k)s, which will require more standardized reporting requirements and greater transparency—but for now, the fine print of fees has a cost that can reach millions.

Private equity investing will always carry a higher cost structure than public markets—that's inherent in its intensely active management model. However, as the industry matures and scales, greater efficiency can drive those costs down over time, ultimately translating into lower fees for investors.

The Liquidity Myth

The second critical factor is liquidity. PE liquidity is more myth than mechanism. Most PE firms will sell you the marketing brochure story of reasonable liquidity—less than publicly traded assets but relatively liquid in a three-to-five-year period where money flows back with returns. This represents an absolute best-case scenario.

In most cases, liquidity extends well beyond the expected timeline—often taking ten years or more to recover invested capital and realize returns. During economic crises, when IPOs freeze up and M&A activity stalls, PE firms' ability to exit investments and return capital becomes severely constrained. Timelines stretch indefinitely.

It is critical to match any PE investment with worst-case liquidity outcomes and overall portfolio needs. Private equity is a poor fit for the short-term investor, due to rebalancing windows, capital calls, and delayed exits. Misreading timelines can force asset sales or create missed market opportunities elsewhere.

To avoid this, align any liquidity strategy to actual PE timelines, not brochure promises, and prepare for less liquidity than communicated. I've seen institutional investors misread liquidity terms, miss crucial rebalances, and compound their risk. There are countless cases of investors who assumed three-to-five-year liquidity, planned their portfolio rebalancing around it, and then found themselves unable to act when the funds weren't available.

Liquidity in PE is earned, not offered. You must understand what the potential ranges of liquidity are, assume the worst end of that range, and then structure your portfolio exposure accordingly.

Hidden Operational Risks

There are also risks that you don't always price out. Operational risk, transparency gaps, and control loss rarely show up in marketing decks. Some PE funds are quite complex and much more aggressive with leverage, and they can end up with more financial restructurings and bankruptcies than other firms.

On average, one in ten portfolio companies go into financial restructuring or bankruptcy. With some of the more aggressive firms, the ratio is one in five. That can significantly increase the complexity of a PE investment—adding restructuring costs, lengthening turnaround timelines, and, in some cases, prolonging bankruptcy proceedings that further delay liquidity. If deals go awry, they can negatively affect your returns significantly. It's very important to understand the exact risk and nature of the actual individual investments within the PE fund that you're investing in.

Lawsuits, bankruptcies, and financial restructurings hit even blue-chip PE portfolios, hurting returns and reputations. Investors may lose more than money—they can lose time, optionality, and trust. Evaluate funds not just on return profile, but governance, track record, and control rights. It's essential to evaluate both the quality and consistency of a PE firm's long-term returns—not just the headline numbers. Look beyond the aggregate performance to understand the nuances of each fund's returns and liquidity profile. Analyze how those elements evolved over time and what truly drove the results.

Why Some Sophisticated Institutions Are Stepping Back

Recently, some pension and endowment funds have reported reducing their PE exposure. Several of the world's most sophisticated pension endowment funds are quietly cutting back on private equity exposure, not because they can't access deals, but because years of underperformance and murky fee structures are no longer worth the gamble. Large institutional investors such as Canada's CDPQ, Ontario Municipal Employees Retirement System, Ontario Teachers Pension Plan, and the Texas Teachers Retirement System have scaled back their private equity commitments after internal reviews revealed a troubling mix of lower-than-expected returns, opaque cost disclosures, and increased operational complexity.

In many cases, headline performance fell short of public-market benchmarks once full fees and carried interest were factored in. The lack of real-time valuation transparency hindered effective portfolio risk management. By reducing direct allocations to PE and favoring co-investments or public-market exposure, these funds seek to improve liquidity, lower costs, and regain greater governance control. This approach better aligns their capital deployment with fiduciary responsibilities and member expectations.

HOW INDIVIDUAL INVESTORS SHOULD THINK ABOUT PE INVESTMENT PORTFOLIO ALLOCATION

For decades, private equity was an asset class reserved for the largest pensions, sovereign wealth funds, and ultra-high-net-worth investors. That exclusivity was part of the appeal, and part of the problem. Most ordinary investors had no access, no visibility, and no way to participate in the kinds of deals that generated double-digit returns for institutions. That wall is starting to crack.

The democratization of private equity is now a live trend. Platforms like Moonfare, Yieldstreet, and iCapital are creating vehicles that allow high-net-worth individuals to buy into private equity funds with minimums far lower than the traditional five-million-dollar ticket. Regulators are also paving the way for smaller individual retail investors: in the US, changes from the Department of Labor and SEC are making it easier for PE funds to find their way into 401(k)s, IRAs, and other retirement plans. The theory is simple—if pensions can benefit from private equity, why shouldn't individual savers?

But access doesn't erase risk. Retail investors face the same issues that institutions grapple with: high fees, low liquidity, and lack of transparency. Once money is committed, it can be locked up for seven to ten years. Valuations aren't marked to market, so investors may not know how their money is really performing until an exit occurs. And unlike institutions, retail investors rarely have negotiating power to push for lower fees or co-investment rights.

The appeal for PE firms is obvious: retail capital represents trillions of dollars that haven't historically been tapped. But for investors, the danger is that they're buying into an asset class without fully understanding the trade-offs. The sales pitch emphasizes higher returns and diversification, but the fine print is often ignored. Illiquidity, complex structures, and the fact that the median PE fund doesn't actually outperform the public markets all matter more when your nest egg is on the line.

The bottom line: private equity is becoming part of the every-day investor's portfolio whether Wall Street is ready or not. For some, that's a positive shift because of access to an asset class that can deliver real diversification and long-term returns. For others, it's a trap; it's a way of locking up retirement capital in high-fee, low-transparency vehicles that are difficult to evaluate or exit. For retail investors, the lesson is clear: treat PE not as a sure bet but as a small, carefully considered slice of a broader investment plan.

Private equity can be an attractive asset class, but it's not for everyone. The right allocation depends on how much wealth you have, how liquid your assets are, and how long you can leave money tied up (I mean truly tied up). Unlike public stocks or bonds, private equity funds typically lock capital away for seven to ten years or more, and that illiquidity can create real problems if too much of your portfolio is committed to the private equity asset class.

Here are some helpful, basic guidelines to follow based on my extensive discussions with experienced wealth managers and my own history with private equity investing:

For investors with **less than $3 million in investable assets**, private equity generally doesn't make sense. The risks, high fees, and long lock-up periods outweigh the benefits. Liquidity and flexibility are far more important at this stage of the wealth ladder.

Once an investor crosses into the **three-to-five-million-dollar range**, a small allocation, around 5%, can be appropriate, but only if the assets are genuinely not needed long-term and are invested through a large, reputable fund house. Even here, diversification is key: private equity should remain a side allocation, not a core holding.

At the **five-to-ten-million-dollar level**, investors can consider increasing to roughly 10%. Retirement vehicles and big fund platforms become more useful here, and a 10-year-plus horizon is critical. Investors in this range should spread their allocation across several funds to avoid being overly dependent on a single strategy or manager.

From **$10–$20 million**, allocations of up to 20% are possible, particularly for those using retirement accounts through established fund houses. Still, liquidity management matters—a strong allocation to public markets and liquid alternatives should remain in place.

In the **twenty-to-fifty-million-dollar tier**, investors often hold both retirement and taxable assets, giving them more flexibility.

Up to 20% in private equity is reasonable here, but the focus should remain on quality PE fund managers, a long-term horizon, and maintaining balance with liquid investments.

Finally, investors with **$50 million or more** move into the ultra-high-net-worth category. At this level, 20% in private equity is still a sensible cap, but access broadens to bespoke opportunities, direct funds, and co-investments. The key here is discipline: even with access to elite managers, investors need to stay focused on fees, risk, and track records rather than chasing exclusivity for its own sake.

The bottom line is that private equity can play a meaningful role in a wealthy investor's portfolio, but only when the allocation matches the investor's wealth level, time horizon, and liquidity needs. And it still requires that you do your homework.

The table below provides a framework, but the principle is simple: the more assets you have, the more you can afford to lock away, and the greater sense it makes to allocate a portion to private equity.

Private Equity Allocation Guidelines
for Individual Investors

Investor Profile	Investable Assets	Suggested PE Allocation	Access & Vehicles	Key Considerations
Mass Affluent	< $3M	0%	Limited access; PE not recommended	Illiquidity, high fees, and concentration risk outweigh potential diversification.
Upper Affluent	$3M–$5M	~5%	Retirement platforms; large fund houses	Use only if assets are long-term; avoid overexposure. Focus on fund house quality.
High Net Worth (Tier 1)	$5M–$10M	~10%	Retirement assets; large fund houses	10+ year horizon essential; diversify across funds rather than one allocation.
High Net Worth (Tier 2)	$10M–$20M	Up to 20%	Primarily retirement assets; large fund houses	Liquidity risk still material; keep public-market exposure for flexibility.
Very High Net Worth	$20M–$50M	Up to 20%	Mix of retirement & taxable assets; various size fund houses	Access improves; still focus on long-term horizon and manager quality.
Ultra-High Net Worth	$50M+	~20% (bespoke possible)	Mix of retirement & taxable assets: Fund houses, direct funds, co-investments, bespoke vehicles	Greater access but discipline still required: fees, risk, and long-term horizon.

KEY CHAPTER TAKEAWAYS

1. Liquidity Isn't a Feature—It Has to Be Earned
- Plan for seven-to-ten-plus years of illiquidity; crises can stretch timelines well beyond brochures.
- Build portfolios so you never need to cash out PE capital in order to address life events or rebalancing.

2. Fees Hide in the Fog
- Judge managers on **net** returns after management fees, carry, transaction fees, and fund expenses.
- Trace fees at both fund-level and portfolio-company level; layered extraction can quietly erase gains.

3. Returns Are Lumpy and Manager-Selected
- The long-run "**+1%–2%** over public markets" average masks wide dispersion.
- Access matters: top quartile is scarce; average funds ≈ average results with higher risk and fees.

4. Diversification Shrinks in Downturns
- Correlations jump in crises—PE behaves more like public risk when you need diversification most.
- Underwrite PE for cycle-aware diversification, not as an all-weather hedge.

5. Liquidity Promises Require Fine Print
- Perpetual or evergreen vehicles can offer periodic gates, not daily liquidity.
- Read redemption terms, gates, side pockets, and suspension rights before wiring funds.

6. Cash Drag and Capital Calls Matter

- Commitments get drawn over time; uncalled capital sitting in cash drags IRR.
- Model commitment pacing and keep a cash plan so you aren't forced to sell public assets at lows.

7. Operational & Governance Risk Are Real

- PE portfolios carry bankruptcy and financial restructuring risk (often cited around one in ten; higher for aggressive styles).
- Evaluate firm governance, control rights, and transparency—not just headline IRR.

8. Retail Access ≠ Retail Fit

- New platforms and 401(k) routes expand access, but illiquidity, fees, and opacity still apply.
- Keep PE a small slice; use reputable platforms and managers, and insist on clear reporting.

9. Set an Allocation You Can Live With

- Practical guideposts: < $3M assets → generally 0%; $3–5M → ~5%; $5–10M → ~10%; $10M+ → up to ~20% max.
- Cap total illiquid alternative investments (PE, private credit, other) to what you can lock for a decade without stress.

10. Model the Downside Like an Owner

- Run scenarios with longer holds, lower exits, fee creep, and delayed distributions.
- Ask: "If distributions slip three to five years, do I still meet goals without forced selling elsewhere?"

Now you know what PE investors wish they had known. But what about sellers? In the next chapter, we walk through how to sell your business to PE without regret.

CHAPTER 13

How to Sell Your Business to PE (Without Regret)

He walked into what he thought was a strategy meeting. It was his last day. This sentence sounds very jarring, but it actually happens. The day after a company transitions into private equity ownership everything changes, and you must fully understand and be prepared for the new dynamics.

In this chapter, you'll learn what every seller must understand about the private equity model before signing so you can protect your role, your vision, and your long-term outcomes. Most founders optimize for valuation, but the smart ones optimize for survivability. The themes in this chapter are essential for any business owner considering—or already in the process of—selling to private equity.

The Fundamental Shift: Your Company Is No Longer Yours

The most important thing to understand is that the day after the sale, it's a different company with a different culture. The change is night and day.

Before the sale, you built and controlled the company—its strategies, its culture, its direction. The day after selling to a PE firm, that control is gone. The culture is different, the strategies shift, and while some may overlap with the past, many will be entirely new. The focus now is on value creation, speed, restructuring, and M&A rollups. Don't fool yourself into thinking it's the same company—it isn't. Accept that reality. You can still play a meaningful, rewarding role in its future, but it will be on different terms, in a different culture, under different ownership.

Protecting Your Position And Equity

You need to protect your money, your equity, and any role you expect to have after the sale. Be crystal clear on the legal parameters of that role—or accept that it will look very different once the PE firm takes over. If you plan to stay on after a PE acquisition, you must understand the acquiring firm thoroughly. Don't leave yourself open to surprises about how they operate, what they expect from the business, or what they expect from you. Misaligned expectations create pain points and fast departures.

Sellers often believe they'll remain in control, but private equity views founders as transitional. Term sheets frequently include clauses allowing immediate leadership changes if targets aren't hit. If you assume trust and stay passive, your influence and equity can vanish.

Before signing, align on role expectations and performance metrics in writing.

The Brutal Reality: A Founder's Cautionary Tale

A founder was blindsided when the PE firm that had just acquired his company replaced him shortly after closing. Before the sale, he led a growing mid-sized oil and gas business with several family members also involved. They sold to a small but aggressive private equity firm for a fixed price, with a large equity earnout tied to future performance and significant ongoing management roles.

After a period of less than twelve months, the founder and his family members were taken out of their roles in the company for cause, which then went to arbitration. Based on the definition of "for cause," they lost their roles and their equity.

This is an extreme example, but it illustrates a crucial point: once you sell to PE and give up control, key decisions—especially around roles and leadership—rest with the PE owners. When it comes to equity, it's essential to have top-tier legal advisors with specific private equity deal experience. Make sure the language around equity and "for cause" is precise and detailed—so you're protected if you leave the company or if something goes wrong after the sale. Carve out a portion of the equity that cannot be taken away under any circumstance.

Your equity is only as strong as your alignment. Know the model or pay the price. And get the right legal advice.

When PE Logic Clashes With Founder Intuition

PE incentives can contradict founder logic, especially when it comes to timelines, control, and culture. PE optimizes for exit value, often through aggressive restructuring and operational and cultural shifts. This goes back to the idea that it's a different company from day one after you sell it to them.

Most business owners aren't in restructuring mode. They're not in overhead-reduction mode, asset-sale mode, or in maximizing-cash-flow mode. They know how to manage cash flow, but they're not making shorter-term decisions to maximize it on an extremely aggressive performance basis. If you don't understand the PE model when you sell, you may be surprised by new initiatives the firm views as value creation: cutting costs, boosting cash flow, selling non-essential assets, and using sale-leasebacks. You could become a frustrated operator in that new environment. Understand the model and the PE firm you're dealing with. Look at their history and operating practices, and make sure you're protected. If you sell without understanding their model, you could feel sidelined in your own company.

Engage specialized legal, tax, and deal counsel—not just a general advisor. A strong valuation doesn't always mean a good fit for you as a business owner. If your goal is simply to sell and walk away, the biggest check may be all that matters. But if you want to stay involved, earn a paycheck, and help shape the company's next chapter, it's not just about valuation. In that case, you'll need to conduct deeper due diligence and think carefully about every legal and structural detail to ensure you're protected for the long term.

WHEN LEVERAGE DESTROYS LEGACY

One business case illustrates the challenges legacy founders and cultures can face when purchased by PE. Bain Capital's leveraged takeover of Gymboree in 2010 piled on massive debt and quietly displaced its visionary founder. This set the stage for an identity crisis and eventual collapse.

When Bain Capital acquired Gymboree in 2010 for $1.8 billion, the children's apparel and play-center company had low debt, was profitable, and had been guided by the legacy of founder Joan Barnes, who had built the brand into a trusted destination for parents. By layering over $1 billion in new debt onto the business, Bain shifted the newly created financial burden onto Gymboree's operations. This drained its strategic flexibility and gradually eroded Barnes's ability to set direction, as financial engineering and debt service took precedence over reinvestment in the brand.

As the financial leverage tightened, Bain's strategy prioritized financial restructuring over organic growth. The firm installed new management and focused on cost-cutting, centralizing decision-making, and accelerating store openings to generate near-term revenue. Marketing budgets were trimmed, product assortments were standardized, and the once carefully curated customer experience began to feel commoditized. Innovation slowed, and Gymboree's ability to differentiate itself from competitors like Children's Place, Gap Kids, and emerging fast-fashion brands was blunted.

At the same time, Bain's debt load limited Gymboree's room to adapt to seismic industry shifts. The rise of e-commerce and discount retailers demanded digital investment and sharper price positioning. Yet Gymboree was hamstrung by interest payments and bond covenants, leaving little capital for technology upgrades or bold strategic pivots. Bain's relentless focus on servicing the debt also meant that underperforming stores lingered too long, while newer concepts cannibalized the brand's identity rather than strengthening it.

Founder Joan Barnes, who had been the creative force behind Gymboree's ethos of playful, high-quality children's fashion, was gradually marginalized. With Bain in control and new executives running the business, Barnes was pushed to the sidelines. Her long-term vision for brand equity and customer loyalty clashed with Bain's financial imperatives. By the time the debt pressure peaked, Barnes had been effectively removed from meaningful influence. The company lost not only its financial footing but also its cultural compass.

The result was inevitable: Gymboree filed for bankruptcy in 2017, restructured, and then filed again in 2019 before liquidating its stores. A once-beloved brand that had thrived debt-free collapsed under the weight of leverage, short-term strategic pivots, and the sidelining of its founder.

The Gymboree case is a stark reminder that leverage can strip a company of its ability to invest, innovate, and remain true to its brand DNA. By displacing the founder's influence and replacing vision with financial engineering, Bain accelerated the company's decline. What looked like a bold buyout in 2010 turned into a cautionary tale of how too much leverage, without the balance of reinvestment and respect for the founder's role, can destroy a legacy brand.

The Power Dynamics Founders Don't See Coming

While most founders vet the PE firm's money, they fail to uncover their methods. Cultural misfits, board dynamics, and micromanagement often catch sellers off guard.

Many sellers don't realize that the PE firm, because it's in control, can make decisions unilaterally. Once a PE firm acquires a company, it may present decisions as consensus-driven, but in disputes over management or performance pressure, the firm ultimately has the power to act as it chooses. Firms can even take the drastic step of getting rid of entire management teams. They can also hire new players and put them in key roles like head of finance or human resources. If things get really bad, they might keep a founder in place as a figurehead, but know that the real power has already shifted.

They may keep specific members of the existing team in certain roles and have their own people in other roles that communicate directly with the PE firm, without going through the normal hierarchical channels. That has happened to me personally as well. In this situation, the PE firm gets two disparate forms of data and communication. Sometimes the leader of the company doesn't even know what kind of information is going to the PE firm. The information may not even be accurate or aligned with what needs to be communicated.

Understand that the PE firm has multiple ways to manage the company and is ultimately in control once the business is majority sold. You may get the price you want but lose the company you built.

The Ultimate Due Diligence: Interview Their Portfolio CEOs

One of the key ways to understand the culture and the operating mannerisms of a PE firm and how they look at driving value in a business is to interview the CEOs of the portfolio-holding companies they currently have. When you interview them, you can quickly see how the firm operates, how it manages and pressures performance, what it does when performance isn't on track, and what kind of operating culture it has.

I've seen situations where sellers have done that due diligence and decided not to sell to a PE firm because they didn't think that the way that PE firm operated and the culture it had at its portfolio companies was a good match for them. Diligence goes both ways if you want staying power.

Interview portfolio CEOs. Ask hard questions. Request governance clarity and understand everything you need to know about the PE firm that's potentially buying your business. You could interview three CEOs from the firm's portfolio, and their brutal honesty may save you from becoming a misaligned partner.

KEY CHAPTER TAKEAWAYS

1. It Isn't the Same Company the Day After
- Selling to PE means your culture and strategy reset overnight.
- Accept that you've sold control—your role will shift whether you like it or not.

2. Protect Your Role in Writing
- Post-close promises are fragile unless legal terms define them clearly.
- Tie role, equity, and earnout protections to objective metrics—not vague trust.

3. Equity Only Matters If It Survives You
- "For cause" clauses can erase both your position and payout.
- Hire specialized deal lawyers who understand PE equity traps, not just M&A basics. Carve out equity that is untouchable.

4. PE Logic Isn't Founder Logic
- PE optimizes for exit speed and value-creation levers—not legacy building.
- Expect moves like cost cuts, asset sales, and cash optimization on day one.

5. Leverage Can Kill Legacy
- Debt loads imposed at buyout can erase flexibility and founder influence.
- Financial engineering can displace vision and lead to collapse.

6. Control Lives With the Firm, Not the Founder
- PE boards can replace you without warning if performance stalls.

- Expect shadow reporting lines and firm-installed executives who answer upward.

7. Diligence Goes Both Ways
- Don't just vet their capital; vet their culture, methods, and pressure playbook.
- Interview portfolio CEOs—their scars reveal more than glossy pitch decks.

8. Valuation Isn't the Only Victory
- The "highest check" isn't always the best outcome if you want to stay.
- Survivability means aligning on fit, governance, and cultural style as much as price.

9. Expect Role Redefinition
- PE firms may sideline founders into figureheads or transition advisors.
- Before signing, decide if you want to fight for a role or cash out cleanly.

10. Get the Right Advisors, Not Just Familiar Ones
- Use counsel who specializes in PE structures, tax traps, and governance terms.
- A great valuation without protection can become a regretful bargain.

Selling to PE is one kind of risk, but there's an even greater one. What you don't see is in the fine print. In the next chapter, we'll explore the red flags most sellers miss and how to avoid losing more than you gain.

CHAPTER **14**

The Red Flags Most Sellers Miss

They were terminated on a Tuesday. By Friday, their equity was gone and no one returned their calls.

This isn't a cautionary tale; it's a pattern. While most sellers focus on valuation and deal terms, they're blind to the warning signs that separate legitimate buyers from predators who view your business as prey. The red flags aren't subtle; they're glaring. But when you're caught up in the excitement of a potential exit, your vision narrows to dollar signs and you miss the signals that should make you run.

In this chapter, you'll learn the most common landmines in selling agreements, from hidden clauses to governance tricks, so you can protect your equity, your team, and your future before it's too late.

Predators vs. Partners

The most dangerous buyers are the ones who move fast and talk big. They promise quick closes, waive due diligence, and make you feel like you've won the lottery. But speed in M&A isn't efficiency; it's desperation. Legitimate buyers with real money take their time because they're building something that lasts. Predators rush because they're running cons that collapse under scrutiny.

Here's what separates the real buyers from the vultures: real buyers ask hard questions about your business model, your team, and your future projections. They want to understand what they're buying. Predators ask soft questions about your timeline, your motivation to sell, and how quickly you need the money. They're not trying to understand your business; they're trying to understand your pressure points. When someone shows up with all cash, no questions, and promises to close in two weeks, you're not looking at your dream buyer. You're looking at your worst nightmare.

The key is that every PE firm operates differently. Before selling your business, conduct deep due diligence on how the firm works and what its culture is. Ask yourself whether their approach aligns with how you want to operate. Once you sell a majority stake, it becomes a different company with a different culture—and the PE firm calls the shots. Be brutally honest with yourself about how things will change and what your role will look like in that new reality.

The Termination Trap That Waits In The Fine Print

The termination trap "for cause" can be redefined after the deal and weaponized. This goes back to the story from the previous chapter. But "for cause" is a mostly generalized situation.

With regard to employment contracts, PE firms have powerful lawyers and are fine with spending significant amounts of money on them to get what they want. If they don't like the way you operate, or they feel like they can get away with getting rid of you "for cause," they'll do it. If you haven't spent a good amount of time and gotten the right advice on the wording around that, it can come back and haunt you.

When you're selling your business to PE and they are keen to do a deal, that's the time when you have the negotiating power to make sure those clauses are in your favor. Many agreements allow for retroactive interpretation of misconduct, incompetence, or nonperformance. If you're terminated "for cause," you can lose all equity and future payout even after years of work. Again, I'm not trying to be overly negative, but there are some extreme cases where the PE firm buys a company with a plan to get the founder out faster than they stated, talked about, or promised.

Sometimes, the PE firm sets up the equity such that the likelihood of it actually paying out is almost zero or extremely low. As a seller, if equity represents a significant part of your company's valuation, you must ensure there are minimum payouts or guarantees that make it truly attainable.

Lock in narrow, clearly defined termination language pre-close and align on arbitration jurisdiction. What sounds like boilerplate can cost you a business.

When Your Equity Becomes A Mirage

Not all equity is created equal, and you may not realize that yours may be structured to vaporize. Preferred shares, liquidation preferences, and capital stacks can leave founders with nothing in a negative exit situation. This highlights the complexity of management or earnout equity plans in a business sale, such as determining whose equity is paid first, how the equity stack is structured, and what criteria must be met before any payouts occur. Targets must be clear, fixed, and account for business factors that could affect them.

A large equity payout may be promised, but with too many structural hurdles or unrealistic targets, the equity becomes a mirage—appearing valuable yet ultimately unattainable. If you don't understand the stack, you're betting blind. Have your equity waterfall modeled under multiple scenarios and negotiate protections. You thought 20% meant upside, but when the exit came, you got zero. The stack can bury you.

There are two types of equity in PE-backed companies. The first is the capital you invest personally, which typically comes with its own ownership level, requirements, and payout structure. The second is performance-based equity—granted for management contribution and results—which follows a different set of terms and payout conditions.

When you invest your own money into a portfolio company, you're often led to believe the worst case is simply earning no return—that your capital will remain safe unless something catastrophic happens. In reality, that's far from guaranteed. As mentioned earlier, as many as one in five PE-backed firms go into financial restructuring or bankruptcy, wiping out investor equity entirely. Even without financial stress, if performance falls short of minimum return thresholds, your investment can still go to zero. The risk of losing your equity is often portrayed as negligible—0%–5%—but in truth, it can be 30% or higher.

The Nightmare Of Becoming A Sidelined Founder

Percentages mean nothing without position. What you own isn't always what you get. Control can shift subtly post-close through board votes, budget approvals, or KPI resets. PE firms often reframe decision-making rights without overtly breaking agreements, and the culture can shift in ways that clash with the founder's original intent. You can end up as a figurehead answering to a structure that no longer respects your values or leadership.

This nightmare scenario unfolds when founders skip due diligence and refuse to be honest with themselves about what the future company culture, business strategy, and value-creation plans will look like. In this scenario, you find yourself struggling to manage and drive initiatives that bear no resemblance to what you thought you were signing up for. But you can't leave. You still want influence, and you're locked into your employment contract and equity earnout.

Now you're trapped in a situation where the PE firm makes all the decisions for you. They've installed a new CFO and other key players who also report directly to them, bypassing you entirely. The board rubber-stamps whatever the PE firm suggests, since their majority stake controls the company anyway. You've gone from lacking belief or excitement in the strategic direction of the company to being completely excluded from the communication and decision-making that drives your business.

The solution? Negotiate protective provisions, board composition rules, and control triggers before close. Clarify what cultural guardrails, if any, will be respected going forward. Don't wait until after a new board vote overrides your budget and you discover you can't reverse it. Don't wait until key cultural rituals and staff priorities have been quietly dismantled while you weren't looking.

When a PE-owned firm hits crisis mode, a founder who fails to secure these protections becomes the most expendable person in the room.

When The Grind Becomes Survival Mode

When performance lags, everything shifts into crisis mode. You find yourself launching wave after wave of value-creation initiatives, trying to get back on track. You warn the PE firm about the risks of cutting marketing budgets, reducing headcount, and selling off key assets—but they decide there's no alternative given the company's results.

As those measures take hold, the focus turns from building a great business to simply surviving. The culture changes. The energy turns defensive, and instead of creating long-term value, you're grinding to protect short-term cash flow.

Control loss rarely feels like betrayal—until it's irreversible. But it's not betrayal; it's by design. That's how PE operates. When performance and exit timing are on track, it can still be intense—full of reporting, reviews, and spreadsheet-driven accountability—but it's also exhilarating. It's capitalism on steroids.

When results slip, however, control tightens. The PE firm steps in more directly, decisions shift upward, and reporting intensifies. The model is built that way; it's how they protect returns. Autonomy fades by design. Your ability to drive your own initiatives shrinks, and you become part of the grind—pushing cash flow and EBITDA in increasingly difficult ways.

KEY CHAPTER TAKEAWAYS

1. Speed Is the Biggest Red Flag
- Real buyers ask hard questions and take time; predators rush and flatter.
- If someone offers "all cash, no diligence, two-week close," it's not a gift—it's a watchout.

2. "For Cause" Clauses Can Be Weapons
- Vague termination language can be reinterpreted after close to cut you out.
- Lock in narrow, specific definitions and arbitration terms before signing.

3. Equity Isn't Always What It Seems
- Stacked preferences and earnout hurdles can turn 20% ownership into zero payout.
- Model your waterfall under multiple scenarios—assume stress, not perfection.

4. The Mirage of Management Equity
- Equity grants without clarity on triggers are worthless promises.
- Demand minimum payouts or guardrails so your upside isn't illusionary.

5. The Silent Creep of Control Loss
- Board votes, KPI resets, and PE-installed executives erode authority quietly.
- Negotiate board composition and decision rights before close, not after.

6. Don't Skip Cultural Diligence

- A buyer's operating culture determines whether you thrive or get sidelined.
- Interview other portfolio CEOs—their scars tell the real story.

7. Figurehead Risk Is Real

- Without protections, you can become a symbol, not a leader in your own company.
- Clarify governance triggers and reserve influence rights during negotiations.

8. Survival Mode Isn't Strategy

- When numbers slip, autonomy disappears—PE grinds for spreadsheets, not vision.
- Protect space for brand, people, and long-term bets before crisis forces cuts.

9. Your Leverage Ends at Signing

- The only time you hold real negotiating power is pre-close.
- Use that window to hardwire protections into contracts—after closing, it's gone.

10. Assumptions Are the Seller's Blind Spot

- Don't assume your role, your culture, or your equity will stay the same post-close.
- Audit what you actually control versus what you believe—assumptions kill deals.

Not every threat comes with a warning label, but in the next chapter, we'll look at a trend reshaping deals altogether. We'll dissect the explosive rise of private credit, and what it means for buyers, sellers, and operators alike.

CHAPTER 15

The Rise of Private Credit (And Why It Matters to You)

You're at a conference when a banker says private credit is the new power player, and no one in the room disagrees.

When learning about private equity, it's essential to also understand private credit because the two are deeply interconnected parts of the same investment ecosystem. Private credit often finances PE buyouts through leveraged loans or mezzanine debt, directly influencing deal structure, returns, and risk. Moreover, many PE firms now operate large credit arms themselves, blurring the line between equity ownership and lending as they seek flexible ways to deploy capital across market cycles.

In this chapter, we'll unpack how private credit has exploded in scale and influence, reshaping deals, shifting power dynamics, and quietly becoming the new gatekeeper of growth and exits.

Let me illustrate just how significant private credit has become—and how rapidly it has evolved into a financial juggernaut.

Over the past decade, private credit has effectively become a new private equity. Today, many PE firms allocate 40%–50% or more of their portfolios to private credit. It has already replaced banks as the primary lender to many private companies and is increasingly stepping in to provide loans to public companies as well.

Like private equity, private credit operates with limited transparency. Its true scale is only broadly understood because it doesn't report like public credit markets. What makes it remarkable isn't just its size but its growing influence—both in normal conditions, as a dominant force on company balance sheets, and in times of financial stress, when that power becomes decisive.

A Short Primer On Private Credit

Private credit refers to lending by non-bank institutions—such as private equity firms, credit funds, or asset managers—directly to companies outside of traditional public bond or bank loan markets. These lenders provide financing that is negotiated privately rather than traded on exchanges, which earns returns through interest payments and fees rather than ownership stakes.

In public credit markets, investors buy bonds issued by companies and have little say in how those companies are run or how the financing is structured. By contrast, private credit investors negotiate directly with borrowers, tailoring loan terms, covenants, and repayment structures to fit specific situations. They often step in where banks can't—or won't—lend, such as in highly leveraged buyouts, financial restructurings, or growth financings.

At its core, private credit is about providing flexible, customized capital (in the form of debt) and capturing the premium versus mainstream lending that comes with illiquidity and complexity.

Private credit returns depend on disciplined underwriting, careful structuring, and managing downside protection through collateral and covenants.

Private credit has expanded rapidly as banks have pulled back from middle-market lending due to more extensive regulation. Many private equity firms have naturally moved into the private credit space, leveraging their deal flow, company relationships, and financial expertise to provide debt capital alongside—or instead of—equity. It allows them to earn steady income, maintain influence over transactions, and participate across the full spectrum of a company's capital structure.

While critics note the rise of "shadow banking" and less transparency in the current surge of private credit, the asset class fills an important gap in modern finance—funding businesses that might otherwise struggle to access credit and offering investors steady, yield-focused returns uncorrelated with public markets.

The New Power Brokers Of Private Equity

In normal times, private credit wields influence on the board and in portfolio-company decisions. But when a PE firm runs into financial distress, can't exit, and must restructure its debt, private credit often steps in as the new owner. Sometimes that means taking a partial stake; in other cases, private credit becomes the majority owner, displacing private equity altogether.

An interesting trend is that many private equity firms, after acquiring a company, bring in the private credit arms of other PE firms to invest in it. As an operator, you may start out running a company for one PE firm—only to see it fall into financial distress, and you find yourself reporting to a different firm that took control through its private credit position. That actually happened to me personally. It is imperative to understand the players that are actually providing private credit to your private equity company's balance sheet. What are their culture and operating paradigms? If things go well, they'll have influence. If things falter, they may have control.

Private credit is quickly becoming the new kingmaker in finance. In many deals, lenders now wield more influence than equity partners. Funds like Ares, Apollo, and Blue Owl control trillions in assets and dictate terms that PE firms once set. Misreading a lender's incentives can derail your deal or distort your strategy. Learn to speak the lender's language—and evaluate their track record, not just their rates.

Sometimes, the private lender's term sheet shapes the transaction more than the PE firms. When a private equity–owned company goes into distress, the private credit providers often become the owners of the company after the financial restructuring. Here's how the power shift works: when you hear "bankruptcy or financial restructuring," no formal bankruptcy law or court proceedings are necessarily going to occur. The PE owners and private credit providers simply get together and come to agreement on who's going to own what going forward. Sometimes the PE firm turns the keys over to the private creditors, and they become the new owners with full equity in the company.

In times of financial stress—amplified by the industry's heavy use of leverage—private credit providers often emerge as the new kingmakers in deals. The borrower is no longer the boss.

The Illiquidity Illusion

Private credit markets often appear stable—until liquidity disappears. When that happens, redemptions can freeze, valuations based on internal models become unreliable, and the lack of transparent pricing can trap investors or delay exits indefinitely.

During financial restructuring, private credit goes through several financial maneuvers on the balance sheet. Payment of principal and interest can be delayed or restructured, fundamentally changing the ultimate investment capital and returns for private credit investors. Like PE, private credit demands rigorous due diligence. Understand not only the history but also the risk profile and the likelihood of stress in the companies receiving those loans.

If you're counting on a smooth refinance or exit, think again. Build optionality into your capital structure and have contingency plans. When credit freezes, watch the portfolio companies scramble when their expected refinancing window slams shut.

When Distress Triggers The Kingmaker Shift

When private credit makes loans to portfolio companies, they have strict covenant rules and payback requirements, just like banks do. When financial stress prevents interest or principal payments, private credit gains leverage; it can manage the refinancing, refuse to refinance and bring in new lenders, or assume the company's equity through financial restructuring.

There are many ways refinancing can be delayed or restructured. Higher interest costs become inevitable because the risk is higher. And when private credit owners become the new private equity owners, they bring a totally different culture and approach to managing the company.

The Management Team Reset

When private credit becomes the new owner and effectively becomes the new PE firm, they typically feel compelled to change management regardless of past performance. Their logic? They are dealing with a company that's been in distress, and part of why it's in distress must be the current management team. In these circumstances, more than 80% of the time the management team changes.

But here's the real kicker: under most financial restructurings, existing equity plans go to zero and there's a total reset of the exit timeline. If the original exit was planned for three to five years, but in year four a financial restructuring makes private credit the new equity owner, the clock resets—and you face another five-year horizon. There aren't many management teams that can survive two cycles with two different PE firms at the same company. It almost never happens.

This should concern you, because it happens far more often than you'd expect. In fact, at some firms, it's become almost routine. Credit confidence is a variable, not a constant. The quiet risk shift in private credit power may offer less transparency and more structural risk than many realize. Covenant-like structures, fast underwriting, and secondary market opacity can expose borrowers to unseen traps.

The Hidden Risks Of Financial Restructuring

When private credit makes its initial investment and issues a loan to a company, the terms are crystal clear—its position in the capital structure, the associated risks, the interest payments, and the expected return on capital. But if stress and financial restructuring follows, all of those certainties can vanish. The debt might actually fall further down in the risk profile, and therefore, the risk of non-payment goes up significantly. The interest may be slashed or spike in the restructuring. All these fundamentals can shift so dramatically that the initial private credit investment becomes completely different from what emerges: a new investment with an entirely different risk profile and return structure.

A misaligned credit partner can do more damage than a bad equity deal, especially when control shifts in financial distress. Treat private lenders like co-owners and treat diligence on their governance as tightly as equity. It's crucial for the business owner who's selling, the investor who's putting money into PE, or the PE-portfolio operating team to understand the details of private credit involvement. What are the rights of the private credit owners? Who's the majority owner? How are they different from the current PE firm? Because this can affect you in the future, especially if the company moves into distress.

One business owner learned too late that his private lender held control rights in times of financial distress—he lost decision authority overnight. The real risk is that when financial stress forces control away from the incumbent PE firm, even long-standing management relationships collapse, and the entire dynamic of the company shifts. Management changes, and the direction of the company changes overnight.

The Convergence Trap

The riskiest partner might not be at the equity table. Blackstone's private credit arm is now larger than many banks, with over $300 billion in credit assets under management. Blackstone has aggressively expanded into direct lending, real estate debt, and infrastructure credit, redefining how deals get funded. PE firms are no longer just equity players. They're your lenders, competitors, and potential acquirers. This convergence shifts leverage. Understand how firms like Blackstone use credit to control deal flow, credit stack risk, and extract value across multiple dimensions.

I observed a founder who unknowingly negotiated with a PE firm that controlled both the equity and the credit side of the balance sheet, losing leverage on both fronts. There are significant examples of firms that take equity and private credit as well. When this happens, the private credit teams still operate differently from private equity teams. They have distinct priorities, risks, and management approaches—separate from those of the private equity holders. But they both feel like they have majority ownership because they're from the same firm. Therefore, the operators of the portfolio company are sandwiched in between the two. It can be an environment where you have even more oversight and more people calling the shots than normal.

Credit isn't a side strategy. It's the new center of power.

WHEN PRIVATE CREDIT BECOMES THE CORE BUSINESS

One of the most striking shifts in private equity has been the rise of private credit—and no firm exemplifies this more than Apollo Global Management. Once best known for its bold, distressed-oriented buyouts, Apollo today generates the majority of its earnings not from equity deals, but from credit and yield-oriented strategies.

In the early 2000s, Apollo's credit business was a modest arm of the firm, focused on opportunistic lending and distressed debt. By the 2010s, it had expanded rapidly into direct lending, structured credit, and insurance-linked assets, using its deep credit expertise and relationships to meet demand from institutional investors hungry for yield in a low-interest-rate environment. The turning point came with Apollo's control of Athene Holding, a large, fixed annuity insurance company, which provided a permanent capital base and steady inflows of assets to be invested into Apollo-managed credit strategies.

This insurance partnership created a self-reinforcing cycle: Athene and other insurers needed safe, income-generating assets to back annuities, and Apollo could originate, structure, and manage exactly those kinds of loans and credit products. Over time, Apollo's credit platform ballooned to become one of the largest in the world. By 2024, Apollo had over $650 billion of its $730 billion-plus in assets under management dedicated to credit and yield strategies, making private credit its dominant business line. Traditional corporate buyouts, once Apollo's calling card, now represent only a minority of its earnings power.

The growth has been driven by multiple forces. Institutional investors—pensions, endowments, and sovereign wealth funds—wanted alternatives to low-yield bonds and turned to private credit funds offering higher spreads. Borrowers, especially midsize companies or sponsors doing leveraged buyouts, sought financing outside of volatile syndicated loan and bond markets, preferring the speed, certainty, and customization of private direct lenders like Apollo. Regulatory tightening on banks after the global financial crisis also opened the door for non-bank private credit lenders to step into markets once dominated by Wall Street. Apollo, with its scale, structuring capabilities, and permanent capital from insurance, was uniquely positioned to capture this shift.

The lesson from Apollo's evolution is that private equity firms can transform their business models when they anticipate structural shifts in capital markets. By building scale in credit, tying it to insurance balance sheets, and offering investors differentiated yield products, Apollo turned what was once a small side business into the core driver of its growth and profitability. In doing so, it reshaped not only itself but also the broader private markets landscape—showing that in the new era, the biggest firms may be less about equity buyouts and more about private credit.

PRIVATE CREDIT VS. PUBLIC DEBT: RETURNS AND DEFAULT DYNAMICS

Private credit has emerged over the last decade as a core part of institutional portfolios (and will soon be part of individual retail investor retirement portfolios), offering higher yields than public debt markets while maintaining default rates that, at first glance, seem surprisingly low. The comparison with public bonds and high-yield debt highlights both the structural appeal and the paradox of the asset class.

Private credit typically generates 10%–12% annualized net returns, well above the 6%–8% historically offered by public high-yield bonds and far higher than the 4%–6% range of investment-grade corporate debt. This premium stems from several factors. Investors are compensated for illiquidity, since private loans are not traded and must often be held to maturity. They also earn a complexity premium, as these loans are bespoke and structured to the specific borrower, requiring intensive underwriting and monitoring. Borrowers themselves are often middle-market companies, unrated and too small for public markets, willing to pay more for capital that can be delivered quickly and flexibly. The presence of private equity sponsors further drives demand for certainty of execution, allowing lenders to negotiate higher spreads.

Given these riskier borrowers, one might expect private credit defaults to far exceed public markets. Yet reported default rates often tell a different story. Traditional measures show private credit defaults of under 1% annually, compared with about 1.5% for high-yield bonds and just over 1% for broadly syndicated leveraged loans. Investment-grade bonds, by contrast, default at less than 0.1% historically. However, if one includes "soft defaults" such as maturity extensions, payment-in-kind interest, or covenant resets, the picture changes. The rating agency Fitch recently estimated that US private credit defaults were running closer to 5% in mid-2025, on par with or slightly above public loan markets once distressed exchanges are included.

Why do defaults appear lower? The explanation lies in how private credit is structured and managed. Lenders conduct far deeper due diligence than is possible in the public bond market, with access to detailed company data and management teams. Loans carry stronger covenants, acting as early warning systems that allow lenders to intervene before a company collapses. Active monitoring, often with monthly or quarterly reporting, keeps lenders close to borrowers. Crucially, most deals involve private equity sponsors, who have strong incentives to inject fresh equity or arrange amendments rather than allow a bankruptcy that could wipe out their investment. Finally, many loans are secured and collateralized, reducing losses even if problems arise.

The bottom line: private credit delivers higher returns than public debt because investors accept illiquidity, complexity, and the risks of lending to smaller borrowers. Default rates appear lower than one might expect not because the borrowers are safer, but because the lending structures, sponsor support, and definitions of default tilt the playing field. The result is an asset class that, while not immune to stress, has proven resilient and lucrative compared with its public-market cousins.

One big watchout. When the next big recession occurs, the weaker private credit deals and players (as well as their investors) will be severely tested.

Reported Returns vs. Default Rates

Private Credit vs. Public Debt: Returns and Default Rates

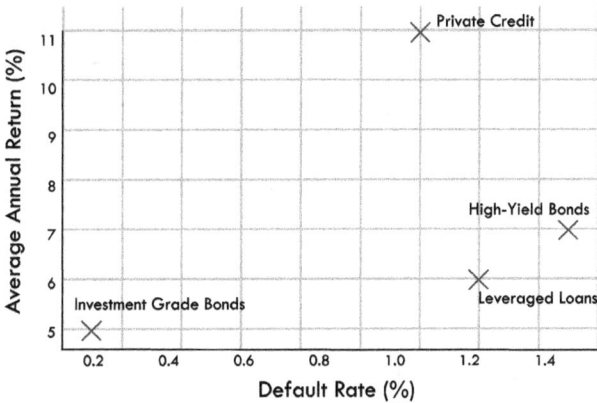

KEY CHAPTER TAKEAWAYS

1. Private Credit Has Become the New Private Equity
- Today, 40%–50% of PE firm capital flows into private credit instead of equity.
- It has quietly replaced banks as the primary lender to private companies.

2. Lenders Are the New Kingmakers
- In financial distress, credit funds often take over equity and control boards.
- If you misread the lender's incentives, you may lose control overnight.

3. Term Sheets Override Equity Promises
- Credit covenants, rates, and control rights often set the deal's true rules.
- Equity only works if your capital structure stays in balance under stress.

4. Illiquidity Isn't Stability
- "Mark-to-model" loans and redemption freezes can mask real risk.
- Build contingency plans for when refinance windows slam shut.

5. Distress Resets the Clock
- When private credit converts to equity, the exit timeline starts over.
- Few management teams survive two full sponsor cycles.

6. Financial Restructuring Rewrites the Deal

- Interest rates, collateral, and even seniority in the debt stack can shift midstream.
- Your "secured" loan or equity may not look the same after a workout (financial restructuring).

7. Management Change Is the Default

- In 80% or more of credit takeovers, the incumbent management is replaced.
- Financial distress makes performance irrelevant—new lenders want new operators.

8. Convergence Creates Conflicts

- Mega-firms (e.g., Blackstone, Apollo) now play both lender and equity owner.
- Operators risk being squeezed between two arms of the same firm.

9. Reported Defaults Understate Reality

- "Soft defaults" (extensions, PIK interest, covenant resets) hide true risk levels.
- Actual stress rates can run closer to 5% or more annually, not the <1% often cited.

10. Credit Isn't Side Capital—It's the Center of Power

- Treat lenders like co-owners, not counterparties.
- Do extensive diligence on their culture, governance style, and crisis behavior before signing.

You now see how private credit can shape, delay, or derail your path. In the conclusion chapter, we'll turn inward and explore what this whole journey has really been about.

CONCLUSION

You did not necessarily start reading this book to master private equity. You wanted to learn how to protect what really matters: your company, your team, your values, your money. But along the way, I hope you found power and clarity.

Private equity isn't inherently good or bad: it's a tool. Like any tool, it can build or break depending on how it's wielded.

This book isn't about fear. It is about fluency. Private equity frequently gets a bad rap, but it plays an important part in the capitalist system—ensuring companies are restructured and made more efficient, and that capital and labor are redeployed to more efficient purposes. It can also be inherently short term and brutal, lacking some of the built-in empathy from broader constituents found in publicly traded companies.

Rather than dismissing private equity, a better approach is to fully understand it, develop the tools needed to succeed with it, and perhaps even improve it. The future of private equity can be better if investors, executives, and entrepreneurs demand it and shape its direction.

That is what I have tried to influence with this book.

Private equity is no longer a niche corner of finance—it's a defining force that shapes companies, careers, and capital itself. Ignoring or even fearing it isn't an option. Throughout this book, you've seen how the game really works—what drives it, who wins, and what it takes to play it well.

This book first revealed what private equity firms truly value and why EBITDA and cash flow sit at the center of everything they do. Fundraising—the lifeblood of the model—sets the pace and pressure for every decision that follows. From there, the book brought the structure of deals into focus, along with the reasons they sometimes unravel even when the numbers look perfect on paper.

Private equity strategy starts with the end in mind. It's reverse-engineered from the exit, not built from the vision forward. Around that framework, powerful but often unseen forces—regulation, ESG mandates, and technology—quietly reshape the game and redefine what value creation means.

A deeper look then revealed the real truth behind PE returns— why net, not gross, performance tells the story. Many deal failures stem not from flawed businesses but from broken processes. Valuation and due diligence can become more illusion than insight when used to justify a narrative rather than challenge it.

Beyond the numbers, the human side of private equity emerged. The importance of building the right team early became clear, as did the cultural shock that follows once PE ownership takes hold. Protecting the human core under relentless performance pressure requires leadership, resilience, and communication as much as financial skill.

The art of the exit came next—how timing, narrative, and discipline ultimately define success. Business owners learned how to sell without selling out their soul. Investors learned about what they wished they had known before committing capital.

In the end, the subtler lessons stood out: red flags rarely wave—they whisper—and private credit is quietly becoming the new power broker, reshaping leverage and control across modern finance.

Private equity isn't just about capital. It's about control, timing, and human judgment under pressure. Understanding how the machine works allows anyone who touches it—operator, seller, or investor—to move faster, think sharper, and navigate it more effectively.

If this book changed how you see private equity, don't stop here. Share what you've learned. Speak it aloud to your team, your partners, and your peers. Do your personal due diligence.

Clarity is power. Now you have both.

If you're an individual, management team,
or company looking to invest in, join, or are already
part of a PE-backed company or fund—and
want to maximize your odds of success—let's talk.

I offer a full range of strategic, consulting, and
coaching services. The investment will be well worth it.

Visit my website, robertfoye.com
(services detailed there); connect on LinkedIn at
linkedin.com/in/robert-foye-883328b9;
or email me at robertfoye88@gmail.com.

Thank you for reading. If this book made an impact on you, I'd be deeply grateful if you left a short review on Amazon. It only takes a minute and means more than you know!

ACKNOWLEDGMENTS

As always, I would like to thank my family, especially my wife Kristi, for supporting me in writing this book. It does take significant amounts of time and mental energy to write a book and get it right. It also takes patience from the people around you, as you endlessly share how well—or how poorly—the book is coming along. Kristi also helped me enormously on edits. She is one of the smartest people I have ever known.

Thank you to my friend Joe Tripodi, whose valuable input greatly strengthened this book. Despite his demanding schedule serving on numerous boards, he generously made the time to contribute, and I am truly grateful.

I would also like to personally thank the team at Author.Inc, my publisher, who made this book possible with their great expertise and capability. Special thanks go to Mikey Kershisnik, Charlie Hoehn, and Miles Rote. They are truly fantastic.

BIBLIOGRAPHY AND FURTHER READING

I have read hundreds of books on private equity, investing, finance (including valuation), and management. Many of the insights from those works have influenced the thinking behind this book. Rather than listing an exhaustive bibliography, I've chosen to highlight ten books on private equity and finance that are particularly worthwhile for readers who want to go deeper.

Appelbaum, E., & Batt, R. (2014). *Private Equity at Work: When Wall Street Manages Main Street*. Russell Sage Foundation.

Cakebread, S. (2020). *The IPO Playbook: An Insider's Perspective on Taking Your Company Public and How to Do It Right*. Wiley.

Coffey, A. (2021). *The Exit-Strategy Playbook: The Definitive Guide to Selling Your Business*. Lioncrest Publishing.

Coffey, A. (2018). *The Private Equity Playbook: Management's Guide to Working with Private Equity*. Lioncrest Publishing.

Damodaran, A. (2012). *Investment Valuation: Tools and Techniques for Determining the Value of Any Asset*. (3rd ed., University Edition). Wiley.

Damodaran, A. (2017). *Narrative and Numbers: The Value of Stories in Business.* Columbia University Press.

Gadiesh, O., & MacArthur, H. (2008). *Lessons from Private Equity Any Company Can Use.* Harvard Business Review Press.

Nayani, U. (2023). *Private Equity Finance Made Easy.* Independently published.

Phalippou, L. (2020). *Private Equity Laid Bare.* (2nd ed.). Oxford University Press.

Sakovska, M. (2022). *The Private Equity Toolkit.* Wiley.

COPYRIGHT PERMISSIONS

PRIVATE EQUITY GLOSSARY OF TERMS

Acquisition Financing: The mix of equity and debt used by a PE firm to fund a company purchase. Often structured to maximize leverage while keeping default risk manageable.

Alpha: Investment returns above a benchmark or expected market return; PE firms market their ability to deliver alpha through active ownership and management.

Alternative Investments: Asset classes outside traditional stocks and bonds, including private equity, venture capital, hedge funds, real assets, and infrastructure.

Asset Stripping: Extracting value from a company through real estate sales, dividends, or cost-cutting, sometimes at the expense of long-term health.

Auction Process: A competitive sale of a company run by investment bankers where multiple PE firms (and strategic buyers) bid for the asset.

Bridge Financing: Short-term financing used to close a deal while long-term debt is arranged.

Buy-and-Build Strategy: A value-creation approach where a PE firm acquires a platform company and then adds bolt-on acquisitions to scale rapidly.

Carried Interest ("Carry"): The share of profits (commonly 20%) earned by general partners (GPs—the PE firm) above a set hurdle rate.

Cash Flow: The actual cash generated by operations, critical for servicing debt and funding distributions.

Clawback: A contractual provision requiring GPs to return excess carry if later fund losses cause overpayment.

Club Deal: A large buyout where multiple PE firms team up to acquire a company, sharing equity and risk.

Continuation Fund: A vehicle that allows a PE firm to move one or more portfolio companies from an older fund into a new one, extending ownership and giving existing investors the option to cash out or roll over.

Control Premium: The added amount buyers pay to gain control of a company compared to its standalone value.

Covenants: Debt terms imposed by lenders (financial or operational) that restrict borrower behavior and protect creditors.

Deal Flow: The stream of investment opportunities a PE firm evaluates, sourced through bankers, advisors, or proprietary channels.

Distribution Waterfall: The hierarchy of payouts from fund returns, typically: (1) return of capital to LPs, (2) preferred return/hurdle, (3) GP catch-up, (4) carry.

Due Diligence: The detailed review of a target company, covering financials, operations, IT, ESG, HR, legal, tax, and regulatory risks.

EBITDA: Earnings before interest, taxes, depreciation, and amortization. The core performance and valuation metric in PE.

Enterprise Value (EV): The total value of a company, including equity and debt minus cash.

ESG (environmental, social, governance): Non-financial performance criteria increasingly demanded by LPs; in PE, ESG initiatives must tie to EBITDA or exit valuation to gain traction.

Exchange Traded Funds (ETFs): An ETF is an investment fund that trades on a public stock exchange and holds a diversified portfolio of assets such as stocks, bonds, or commodities.

Exit: Realization of returns in a company through a sale, IPO, secondary, or recapitalization. Timing is often the most critical driver of value.

Financial Engineering: Use of leverage, dividend recaps, and structuring to amplify returns without relying solely on operational improvements.

Fundraising: The lifeblood of PE; GPs raise capital commitments from LPs every three to five years, based on prior fund performance.

General Partner (GP): The PE firm, which manages funds, executes deals, and earns fees and carry interest.

Growth Equity: A hybrid between venture and buyouts, investing in minority stakes of expanding companies with proven models.

Hurdle Rate: The minimum return (often 8%) before carry is paid.

Initial Public Offering (IPO): Taking a company public, often as an exit.

Internal Rate of Return (IRR): The annualized return on an investment, highly sensitive to exit timing.

J-Curve: The early negative returns in PE funds (due to fees and early costs) before exits generate positive returns.

Key Performance Indicator (KPI): A KPI is a quantifiable metric used to evaluate how effectively a company, team, or individual is achieving key business objectives.

Key Person Clause: A contractual protection for LPs; if key GP leaders depart, fundraising or investing may pause.

Letter of Intent (LOI)/Term Sheet: Preliminary legal agreement in a company acquisition outlining price, structure, and exclusivity before confirmatory diligence.

Leverage: Debt used in a buyout, often pushing company debt levels from ~20% (public companies) to 50% or more under PE ownership.

Leverage Buyout (LBO): The hallmark PE deal structure: acquiring a company using significant debt, to be repaid with company cash flow.

Limited Partner (LP): Investors in PE funds (pensions, endowments, sovereign wealth, family offices, wealthy individuals).

Management Buyout (MBO): When a company's management team partners with a PE firm to acquire their own business.

Management Equity Plan (MEP): A program that grants and/or sells ownership equity to a company's management team, aligning their interests with the PE firm.

Management Fees: Typically 2% annually on committed capital, paid by LPs to cover GP expenses.

Margin Expansion: Improving profitability by raising prices, cutting costs, or improving efficiency.

Mark-to-Model: A valuation method used when market prices are unavailable, relying instead on internal financial models and assumptions to estimate an asset's value.

MOIC (Multiple on Invested Capital): MOIC measures the total value generated by an investment relative to the amount of capital originally invested.

Multiple Expansion: Selling a company at a higher EBITDA multiple than it was purchased at, a key driver of PE returns.

Net IRR: Investor return net of all GP fees and carry.

Non-Bank Financial Institution (NBFI): A financial entity that offers lending, investment, or insurance services but does not hold a full banking license and generally cannot accept demand deposits. Examples include insurance firms, leasing companies, microfinance institutions, and investment funds (including private credit funds).

Non-Deposit-Taking Financial Institution (NDFI): A subset of NBFIs that provides credit or financing services without accepting deposits from the public. Examples include leasing companies, factoring firms, and private credit funds; all NDFIs are NBFIs, but not all NBFIs are NDFIs, since some NBFIs are authorized to take limited deposits.

Operating Partner: Senior executives embedded by PE firms in portfolio companies to drive operational improvements.

Operational Improvements: PE-led initiatives (supply chain savings, IT upgrades, digital transformation, headcount changes) to boost EBITDA.

PIK Interest (Payment-in-Kind Interest): A form of interest payment where the borrower pays interest with additional debt or equity instead of cash.

Platform Company: The initial acquisition in a buy-and-build strategy, used as a base for add-ons.

Portfolio Company: Any business owned by a PE fund.

Preferred Return: The guaranteed minimum LP return (usually 8%) before carry flows to GPs.

Private Credit Fund: A non-bank financial institution (NBFI) that uses investor capital to lend directly to companies, often in the middle-market or sponsor-backed space. It does not take deposits but serves as an alternative lender, offering flexible financing to borrowers and higher yields to investors.

Public-Market Equivalent (PME): A performance metric that compares a private equity fund's returns to a public-market index over the same time period.

Quality of Earnings (QoE): An audit-style review validating that reported EBITDA reflects true recurring profitability.

Quick Ratio: A liquidity measure sometimes used in diligence to test short-term solvency. It includes cash and cash equivalents, marketable securities, and accounts receivables.

Recapitalization ("Recap"): Restructuring a company's debt and equity mix; dividend recaps allow PE firms to extract cash pre-exit.

Roll-Up Strategy: Acquiring multiple smaller players in a sector to achieve scale and synergies.

Secondary Market: The trading of LP fund interests or the sale of portfolio companies to other PE firms.

Sponsor: Another term for a private equity firm leading a buyout.

Term Sheet / Letter of Intent (LOI): Preliminary legal agreement in a company acquisition outlining price, structure, and exclusivity before confirmatory diligence.

Timeline (Holding Period): The average PE ownership period of three to seven years, driven by fund cycles.

Transition Service Agreement (TSA): A short-term contract between a buyer and seller outlining services the seller will continue providing after a deal closes—such as IT, HR, or accounting support.

Valuation Multiples: Shorthand (e.g., "10x EBITDA") for pricing companies in deals.

Value-Creation Plan: A roadmap drafted before closing to improve operations, cut costs, and begin EBITDA growth immediately.

Venture Capital: VC invests in early-stage, high-risk startups.

Vintage Year: The year a fund is raised; key in benchmarking returns across funds.

Waterfall: Distribution structure dictating how cash flows from portfolio companies are split between LPs and GPs.

Working Capital Adjustment: A post-closing true-up ensuring the company's short-term assets/liabilities are normalized at sale.

Zero-Based Budgeting (ZBB): ZBB is a budgeting method in which every expense must be justified for each new period, starting from a "zero base."

Zombie Fund: A fund beyond its stated life that struggles to exit assets, often delivering poor returns.

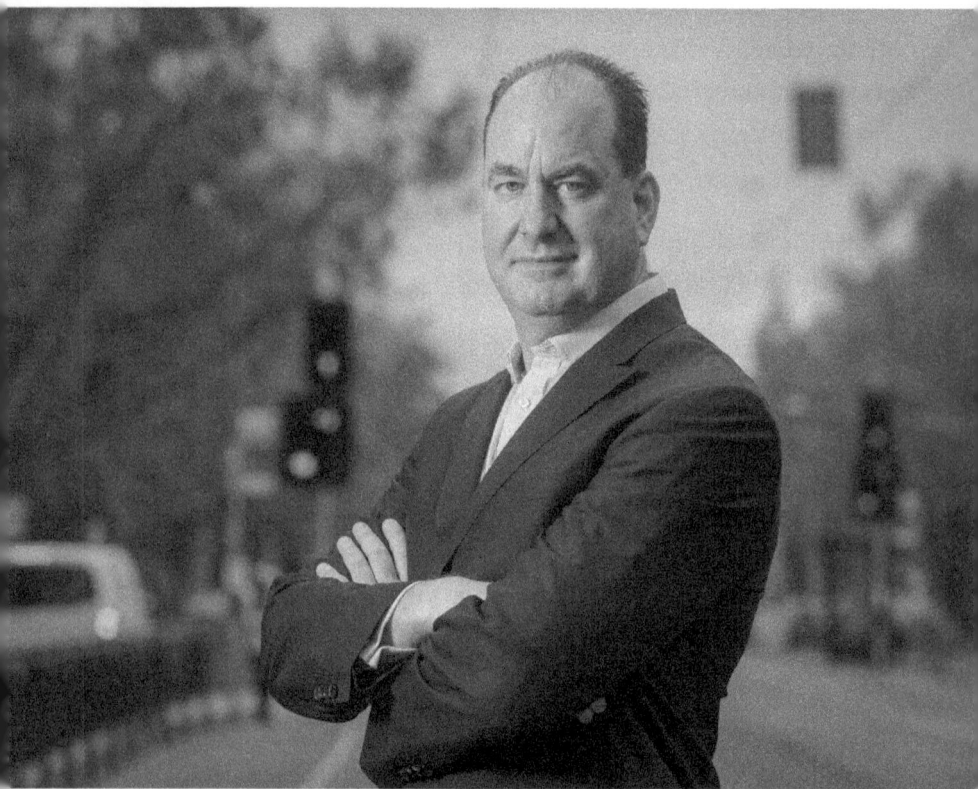

ABOUT THE AUTHOR

Robert Foye is the former Chief Executive Officer (CEO) of Accolade Wines, the largest Australian wine company, which was owned by the Carlyle Private Equity Group. He also previously served as the global Chief Operating Officer (COO) of Treasury Wine Estates, the world's largest publicly traded wine company, headquartered in Australia. Prior to that, he spent twenty-two years with The Coca-Cola Company, working across Asia, Europe, and the United States. He also has worked for Deloitte & Touche as a general management consultant and for Warburg Pincus as an advisor.

He has been a passionate investor for more than thirty years, with particular interest and experience in private equity.

Mr. Foye graduated from Rice University in Houston, Texas, earning a BA in Political Science in 1988 and an MBA in Finance and Accounting in 1990. He has also earned CPA, CFA, and CMA designations.

He currently teaches a second-year MBA course on private equity at the University of Houston's Bauer College of Business.

Robert grew up in Houston, Texas, and West Point, New York. He previously lived overseas in Asia, Europe, and Australia for twenty-three years. He is an avid basketball player, weightlifter, and tennis enthusiast. His other interests include reading, watching movies and TV series, and traveling. A devoted wine lover, he is married to Kristianna and they have four children: Robert, William, Meredith, and Annabel. He currently resides in Houston, Texas.